The Journey Blueprint
Following the Hero's Path to Take Control of Your Life Story

Julie M. Bouché

ISBN-13: 978-0692132562 (Decision Point Books)
ISBN-10: 0692132562

DEDICATION

To all those who have helped, mentored, and
walked with me on my own Journey.
You are in this book and in my heart.

CONTENTS

For additional resources and free downloads, visit us at

thejourneyblueprint.com

A JOURNEY OF MY OWN

We must be willing to let go of the life we planned so as to have the life that is waiting for us.

—Joseph Campbell

In the summer of 2010, my husband and I were forced to close down the small business he and his brother had started. Opening just before the economic recession of 2008 hit with full impact, the business had never made it to breaking even, let alone being profitable. Month after month the debt was deepening, and we were finally forced to accept that the venture had failed.

The next three years were full of difficulty, frustration, and heartache. Saddled with more than $100,000 in debt, he and I struggled desperately to keep our heads above water. He worked overtime and I worked several part-time teaching jobs, all while raising three young children. As a family, we sacrificed, made difficult decisions, and had painful conversations.

Amidst this already difficult time, I suffered a miscarriage, the

i

company my husband worked for went under, and extended family struggles continued to deepen and impact our lives. It was a dark time for us; most of the time it felt like we couldn't even see the tunnel, let alone the light at the end of it.

In 2012, I was teaching English for a school housed in a residential treatment center for women suffering from eating disorders. As much as my previous students had enjoyed and found value in the Hero's Journey as a way to look at literature, this group was different. One girl in particular was very focused. She had been a patient at the facility in the past and had relapsed a few short months after returning home. Now she was back in treatment, struggling to overcome not only the difficulties of her eating disorder, but also her perceived "failure" at having to come back after she believed she had recovered.

We were nearing the end of the lesson, talking about the Return phase of The Hero's Journey, and she was scribbling notes furiously—more notes than I had asked them to take. We talked about the final examples and I asked if there were any questions. She stared at the board, her brow furrowed in concentration. Suddenly, she dropped her pencil and leaned back in her chair, exclaiming, "Bouché, I finally get what happened."

She went on to explain how her own life matched what we were talking about, and that she saw in herself one of the dangers of the Return phase playing a part in her relapse—a situation she was determined to not repeat. This was about more than just a recognition of the concepts; understanding these principles gave her the power to change her own story.

In that moment, it occurred to me that I had been encouraging my students to see the connections between the Hero's Journey and their own lives in a clinical, almost "Isn't that neat?" kind of a way. It had not occurred to me that knowing about these steps was anything more than informative.

Now, however, I could clearly see that this knowledge was not only interesting, it was functional. People could do more than just see the steps in their own lives, they could use that knowledge to actually change their lives. Knowing about Journeys was not just interesting, it was empowering.

This moment of realization showed me how my experience of the Journey I was living could be different. Instead of fighting the process, I could embrace it. Instead of insisting that I had to do it alone, I could open myself to those who were ready and willing to help. Instead of making the same mistakes over and over, I could focus on listening and learning. I had to let go of the life I had planned to truly live the life that was waiting for me.

My experience in coming to see this process in my life has changed me for the better. Not just that specific Journey I was on when I gained this understanding, but all the Journeys since. Each time I allow myself to not only experience the Journey, but also to reflect on the truths that the Journey itself teaches, I come closer to the best version of myself.

The ideas presented in this book have the ability to change the way you experience your Journeys in the same way they have changed me. They can give you power and hope when both seem in short supply. They can help you break free of vicious behavioral cycles, or start you moving forward if you're feeling stuck or lost. They can help you connect with those around you as well as the larger forces that are invested in your personal growth and welfare. Most of all, they can allow you to live your life as the amazing adventure it is intended to be.

We are all on Journeys, whether we want to be or not. Now is the time to start living like it.

"It's time to become the Hero of your Journey."

NOTES BEFORE WE START

Vision is knowing who you are, where you're going, and what will guide your journey.

—Ken Blanchard

This book is the culmination of more than a decade of teaching Joseph Campbell's ideas about the Hero's Journey, as well as coming to understand how change works and how we can take control of our stories. The concepts, as well as their power, have grown and developed for me over the years. Campbell's ideas acted as a foundation for me upon which other thinkers and writers have built and expanded my understanding—teachers who appeared as I became ready. As I live through these Journey experiences, my understanding of the pattern deepens and evolves, as does the way I teach or speak about it. This constant developing, this fine-tuning, keeps me hungry for more, learning something new each time I have the opportunity to share with others.

As what I will present is built upon Campbell's ideas, but different from his original Hero's Journey, when speaking of the process as I have identified it I will use the phrase "Journey Model." The end result is, I hope, not only respectful to the original ideas, but also honors the experiences and insights that have expanded on those ideas and taken them to a personal level.

I wrote this book with the intention that it be read from beginning to end at least once in order to get the full picture of the Journey Model. The Journey is a process, and the phases happen in a relatively certain order. However, once you understand the Journey as a whole, returning to the book to read specific sections that apply to your current situation can be just as powerful as reading the book in its entirety.

I recommend keeping a journal with you as you read, though this is clearly optional. Each chapter will have reflection questions and things to consider. You can simply reflect on your answers, but taking the time to write your answers to these questions will help you identify how these phases and steps manifest in your life. These prompts will be found in the boxes titled "Before You Move On."

Each chapter starts with a literary example, followed by explanation of the concepts, at which point I have put prompts in that focus on literature and stories. Immediately following those question, there is a biographical example (labelled "Real-World Journeys"), followed by personal application, and finally personal application questions. This format runs through each of the main chapters.

There is a blank template at the end of the book (see page 141) that you can use as you read. If you follow the figures included in the chapters, by the end of Chapter 9 you will have a completed version of the basic Journey Model.

Please know that, as much as I have chosen examples that have been the most helpful to diverse groups of students over the years, there are (literally) millions of other examples that would have been just as illustrative. The examples were chosen because of familiarity, separate from any literary merit or societal importance. I try to give enough context to explain how the examples demonstrate the concepts, even if you are not familiar with the book or the movie. Please know that I will be discussing plots in detail, which means if you are not familiar with these stories I will be telling you what happens (i.e. SPOILER ALERT!). If you don't want any spoilers, feel free to skip the sections that talk about the literary examples.

Beyond the examples I use to illustrate the concepts, I encourage you to choose your own favorite characters to walk with you on this Journey, and to see how their stories compare with your own. Learning to listen to the truths in the Journeys around us opens us up to numerous priceless insights and understandings—insights and understandings that connect and empower us to take just one more step. And then another. And then another.

My hope for all those who read this book is that you start to see these patterns in your own life. Once you can see them, I hope you find in the process the power that you have as the main player, the Hero, in your own personal Journey.

As a warning: knowing about these ideas will not suddenly make you successful or attractive or grant superpowers. Believe me, I wish it did. What it will do is show you very clearly what you can and cannot expect or control in this Journey called life, and where you have the power to change the outcome of your story.

To take control of your story, through good times and bad. To be able to look your challenges in the eye, to see them for what they are, to call them by name, and to face them with a knowing smile. To embrace this process in a way that sets you free to live a life so much more than you could imagine. This is my call to you.

It's time to become the Hero of your Journey.

1. AT THE VERY BEGINNING

It was a quiet morning, the town covered over with darkness and at ease in bed. Summer gathered in the weather, the wind had the proper touch, the breathing of the world was long and warm and slow. You had only to rise, lean from your window, and know that this indeed was the first real time of freedom and living, this was the first morning of summer.

—*Dandelion Wine* by Ray Bradbury

The story of the Hero's Journey is as old as stories themselves. It stretches across countries and cultures and can be found in almost every single piece of storytelling in the world today. The pattern itself is relatively simple: the Hero receives a call to go on a Journey, leaves home, does something difficult, and returns home a changed person. That's it.

And yet, we find ourselves drawn to these stories again and again even though we have some sense as to how the story is going to proceed before we even begin to read. It's as though we are looking for something when we engage with these stories, something more than just entertainment.

We each have particular stories that move us, change us, in ways that we don't always understand. This is particularly strange because the stories themselves are, at their core, similar to so many other stories. Perhaps it is that similarity that draws us to them—not just similarity to other stories, but to *our* story specifically.

We experience Journeys in our own lives each and every day. We are called, leave home, do something difficult, and come back changed. Being drawn to stories that resonate with ours, that give us insight into our own struggles, may explain why we were moved by a story even if others were not. There is something powerful in story, something more complex and subtle than most of us realize: the power of connecting the story to ourselves.

DEFINE: JOURNEY

Before we launch into this process, let's take just a second to define what we mean by "Journey" in the context of our discussion. A Journey is a very specific type of experience, and I want to make sure we are all on the same page.

Journeys are experiences where the Hero is forced to engage with the world outside of their comfort zone. They are asked to do things that are difficult for them, where failure is very real and likely. The Journey is a process of growth, seeing the Hero transform into something more than they were before because of all they've learned and all they've had to sacrifice.

In addition, Journeys are ultimately focused on internal improvement. While earning a great deal of money or conquering a neighboring empire may include the things listed in the paragraph above, if there is no moral progress for the Hero, no refining of character, it is not a Journey. It is a project.

Journeys may take the Hero far and wide, or they may happen in a character's own home. Distance travelled does not matter. If all the character does is travel from one place to another without being changed by the experience, it is not a Journey. It is a vacation.

With these characteristics in mind, let us take our first look at the Journey Model.

ONCE UPON A TIME

Let us begin, then, with our own "Once upon a time"—the moment we allow a story to take us from where and when we are into the world of the story. We get to join the Journey of its characters, seeing what they see, experiencing what they experience. Before that happens, we have to be introduced to the world that we are entering.

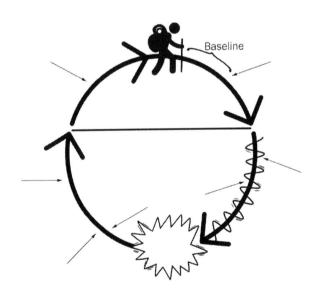

If we were to diagram this first step, we would see that it comes before the real action of the story begins. In these initial paragraphs or scenes, we are given a glimpse into the life and the world of the Hero of the story, establishing not only who they are, but the circumstances that they are living in.

This also includes any rules that the Hero and their world operate within. If there is magic in their world, we are introduced (if only briefly) to the rules of that magic. If the government of their world is a dictatorship, we learn the rules that govern their tyranny. If the Hero is in any relationships, we establish the rules of those relationships, whether they are healthy or dysfunctional. Sometimes the Hero is not even aware of the rules on a conscious level, but as we dig into the background information, we begin to see these rules and the impact they have on the Hero and their world.

This information is important to us, as outsiders, to help us establish a base of information that we can build upon. Places are described, characters are introduced, and enough relevant information is given to allow us to follow what is going to happen to the Hero.

This idea of getting background information seems simple enough; after all, we need to have a context in which to understand what is happening. In many ways, however, we are doing something a bit more subtle: we are establishing a baseline. The characters we meet at the beginning of the story are not the same characters we will see at the end of the story. The initial information we receive not only helps to orient us to the world we are entering, it also acts as a measuring stick of sorts, allowing us to see the change and progress that the Hero experiences as they move through the Journey.

What makes analyzing stories so interesting for someone like me is this process of discovering patterns and relationships that we otherwise miss if we don't take the time to look for them. The Journey Model is one of those patterns, and we will see as we work through the different examples that the similarities often start right at the beginning. In this case, there is a similarity in this "beginning state" across thousands of stories for thousands of characters.

What is the state of so many at the beginning of their stories? Can you think of any examples from stories you are familiar with? Generally speaking, the Hero is in a state of discontent. There are a couple of exceptions to this (that will be discussed in Chapter 10), but generally stories start with the character being, in some form or another, unhappy.

This unhappiness exists on a spectrum. On the one end of the spectrum, the Hero may be bored, listless, or tired. On the other end, they may be in actual, literal danger, existing in some life-threatening situation. Between those two extremes are countless variations and gradations, but it all boils down to the Hero being in an external or internal (or both) place where things are not okay. The Hero either desires a change or a change is coming (whether they want it to or not). This tension is causing the Hero to feel uneasy at the very least.

Perhaps a few examples will help to illustrate how this state of discontent can appear:

Katniss Everdeen (*The Hunger Games*) lives in a world of deprivation, fear, and uncertainty as she awaits the annual Hunger Games drawing.

Samwise Gamgee (*The Fellowship of the Ring*) dreams of meeting elves and seeing other fantastic sights—sights that are well outside the realm of possibility in the quiet life of the Shire.

Harry Potter (*The Sorcerer's Stone*) is an orphan (which, from an archetype standpoint, automatically makes him a "sad" character) living with his abusive uncle, aunt, and cousin. All he longs for is love and belonging, neither of which are available to him in the Dursley home.

Luke Skywalker (*Star Wars: A New Hope*) wants nothing more than to leave and go find adventure in the world outside the moisture farm on Tatooine.

Andy Dufresne (*The Shawshank Redemption*) has been sent to prison for a crime he did not commit: the murder of his wife.

Pi Patel (*The Life of Pi*) spends the first fifteen chapters discussing points of conflict in his life: kids making fun of his name, the conflict between his father's view of zoos and the view of zoo-goers, and ultimately his decision to study both religion and zoology, trying to bring together two seemingly incompatible worlds.

Moana Waialiki (*Moana*) is striving to become the leader her people will need and to find contentment on her island, but finds herself called to the ocean, much to her family's chagrin.

Frodo Baggins (*The Lord of the Rings Trilogy*) has spent his entire life being torn between the quiet life of the Shire and the adventures that live in the stories of his uncle Bilbo.

Are you starting to sense the pattern? Over and over we find characters who are, for various reasons, unhappy with their current circumstances.

As we are given a glimpse into the world we are entering, as we start getting to know the characters and the circumstances causing this discontent, we may feel that the reason the character is unhappy is completely understandable and relatable. On the other hand, we may see these feelings as unwarranted, petty, or self-inflicted.

What matters is not necessarily why the character feels the way they do. What matters is the feeling itself, and the impact these feelings will have on the character's willingness to embark on the Journey that waits for them.

Before You Move On:

Take a moment to consider some of your favorite stories. What is the beginning situation for the main characters in these stories? Are they unhappy? Oblivious? Tormented? Bored? Consider the establishment of the baseline for that character. What do we know about them? About their world? About the circumstances that they are living in? What rules are they subject to?

"*The start of a Journey will often begin with some form of emotional discontent.*"

The beginning is the hardest part to overcome. To decide that you will live the life of your dreams can be a scary undertaking but worth it nonetheless. Begin now, beyond your fear, and create your new life.

—Avina Celeste

REAL-WORLD JOURNEYS

Because the purpose of this book is to not only demonstrate the principles in stories, but also help relate them to ourselves, the next step is to discuss how these concepts could manifest in our lives.

We have all been on Journeys—many of them, in fact. The first day of school, going to summer camp, starting to learn a sport or an instrument, changing jobs—experiences of these types can all count as Journeys. As such, we would be well-served by establishing baselines for ourselves, as well as examining the rules or boundaries we live within.

Establishing a baseline is common practice in science, business, health, education, and other disciplines. Baselines serve as a point of reference that allows us to measure progress and change. Without a baseline, we have no sense of whether or not we have moved in any direction, let alone moved in the direction we desire. Taking the time to figure out where we are seems so simple—maybe even too simple—but skipping this part of the process leads to confusion and frustration.

So how do we go about figuring out where we are? In life, we don't have the luxury of a narrator giving us the baseline information that sets the scene for our future changes. Instead, we have to learn to find the (often) subtle signals that tell us we are at the beginning.

Much like the characters in the stories discussed, the start of a Journey will often begin with some form of emotional discontent. In fact, it is our emotional state that is usually the key to recognizing the initial step of the Journey. Emotions that are typical include boredom, frustration, anxiety, or yearning. Emotions that demonstrate a tension, even if that tension is healthy or positive in nature, are a good sign that something is coming.

One of the most powerful benefits of understanding the Journey Model is being able to recognize the signs that indicate which phase or step of the Journey we are in. If we are aware of the emotional signals, we can start looking at the ways that we personally manifest this initial step. We have the power to recognize these emotions and behaviors as indicators, as messages to be listened to. The sooner we recognize our indicators of this state of discontent, the sooner we can prepare for the possibility of change.

In addition, it is always a helpful exercise to examine the rules that we consider ourselves subject to, especially internal rules. External rules (such as laws, regulations, codes of conduct, etc.) are important to understand. More than that, however, we need to look at the rules or boundaries we place upon ourselves, often arbitrarily and subconsciously. Do we have rules about what is right or appropriate? Rules about money? Rules about asking for help? The more we uncover these internal rules, the more open we can be to changing them.

Before You Move On:

Take some time to consider an experience you have had with a Journey in the past, or one that you are currently experiencing. Reflect on the following questions:

- What were the rules that defined your world?
- Were those rules spoken? Were there any unspoken rules?
- What was your physical/emotional/mental state before you started the process?

2. CHANGE IS COMING

It's time for the drawing. Effie Trinket says as she always does, "Ladies first!" and crosses to the glass ball with the girls' names. She reaches in, digs her hand deep into the ball, and pulls out a slip of paper. The crowd draws in a collective breath and then you can hear a pin drop, and I'm feeling nauseous and so desperately hoping that it's not me, that it's not me, that it's not me.

Effie Trinket crosses back to the podium, smoothes the slip of paper, and reads out the name in a clear voice. And it's not me.

It's [my sister] Primrose Everdeen.

—Katniss Everdeen, *The Hunger Games* by Susanne Collins

Establishing a baseline for our character only matters because we know something is going to happen: a change is coming. The character, already existing in this state of discontent, is going to receive an invitation to go on a Journey. This invitation is referred to by Joseph Campbell as a "call to adventure," though there are other names and designations that can also be used. Regardless, *the Call* (as we will refer to it here) indicates the first interaction between the Hero and what is to come.

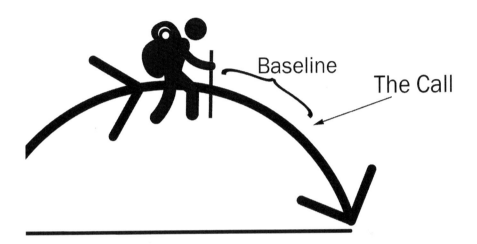

THE DIRECT INVITATION

Calls can, like all the other steps, take on many forms. The most obvious version is the *Direct Invitation*. For some characters, the Call is a literal call—a phone call, a letter, an invitation to a party, etc. The Hero is directly invited to do something. These types of Calls are pretty easy to spot as you look for them. What the Hero is being invited to do is usually clearly outlined.

A letter from a wizarding school inviting future students to attend would be an example of a Direct Invitation, as would a college acceptance letter, or an offer for a lunch date to talk about a new opportunity. The Invitation is clear, and the expected response from the Hero is also clear.

THE INDIRECT INVITATION

Calls are not always as literal, though. With an *Indirect Invitation*, the Hero may experience a Call that may not seem like a Call at all. The Hero may see a job listing in the newspaper that seems interesting or find a different route home than the one they normally take. Perhaps they expected an invitation of some sort but didn't get one, or they encounter the same person in their village every day and feel a desire to know more about them.

Indirect Invitations can be less easy to spot, as the expected reaction of the Hero is not clearly defined. Instead, these types of Calls represent potential or possibility. What the Invitation is and how the Hero should act can be unclear.

THE MANDATE

Still other Calls take an even more intangible form. There may be a sudden illness diagnosis, or an unexpected death in the family. Perhaps someone new moves in next door, or mankind learns that an asteroid is headed on a direct collision course with the earth. These Calls are less invitations (where the Hero generally seems to have a choice) and more like announcements that the world the Hero knows is going to change. Change is not really optional for these Heroes, and for this reason we call these types of Calls *Mandates*.

Mandates often come in the form of decisions made by other people that impact the Hero. This can be an abuser, a tyrant, an evil force. This can also be a loving parent, a mentor, a boss. The intentions of the "other" in this case do not matter as much as the impact their decisions have on the Hero. A tyrant who enslaves the Hero's people produces a Mandate for the hero to deal with. So too, however, does the loving parent who gets a new job that requires the family to move, pulling the Hero from the world they know and love. Generally, these decisions put the Hero on a path that they would not choose for themselves, regardless of whether the experience is positive or negative.

Mandates are often "points of no return" where, regardless of how much the Hero wishes it were otherwise, there is no going back from the changes. There is no way to go back from a death, or an illness diagnosis. Nor is there a sane way to deny these realities. The world has changed; the question is how the Hero will deal with the change?

THE SOURCE OF CALLS

So where exactly do these Calls come from? We can break this idea down into two basic categories.

The first category is a character or player within the world of the character. These could be people, penguins, bears, aliens, etc., but ultimately, we can put a finger on who (or what) originated the Call. We see that both Invitations and Mandates can come from this type of source.

The second category is less simple to define. One of the easiest ways to conceptualize this source is to refer to it as Fate or Destiny, though even that can seem a bit simplistic. Often in stories we could see things like coincidence or luck impact the Hero and send them on a Journey, though we aren't sure the source of those influences. This category, as difficult as it is to define, encompasses the unseen force that affects the Hero's life, but that seems to have an interest in the character going on a specific Journey—an experience that we know is intended for the betterment of the Hero.

A WORD ABOUT FATE OR DESTINY

Regardless of the role Fate or Destiny plays in the Call, all Journeys seem to have a greater force involved in the overall process. The alignment of events, the preparation of Heroes, the persistent push toward an individual's improvement in the midst of sometimes world-changing events, all suggest something much more planned and intentional than "just coincidence."

So, look for the influence, the "fingerprints," of these greater forces in the stories. All the way through the process there will be specific people, events, experiences, etc., that seem to be exactly what the Hero needs at just the right time.

BEFORE SHE WAS THE MOCKINGJAY

Katniss Everdeen, from the *Hunger Games* series, has an interesting Call that illustrates a couple of different elements that can come into play. As someone who has grown up in a difficult world, Katniss is a tough, guarded character. Living in the dystopian world of Panem, the entirety of District 12 struggles to find enough food, forcing Katniss to knowingly break the law to provide for her family. The leadership of Panem, stationed in the Capitol, rules with fear and intimidation. The threat of violence keeps people constantly looking over their shoulders, worrying if something they do or say will bring retribution down upon them. This is Katniss' baseline, and it is very clear that a change is needed.

For Katniss, the event that draws her out on her Journey is an annual one: The Hunger Games. This event is anticipated, it is familiar, and it is, for all intents and purposes, inevitable. There is no surprise that the representatives of the Capitol will come to each District, that children ages twelve and up will have their names entered in the lottery, and that the entire town will have to come and line up and listen for the names to be drawn. This same event happens every year across all the Districts in Panem.

Those whose names are drawn will be forced to compete for their lives in the hopes of not only being the sole survivor but bringing some relief to the people suffering in their District as well. The inhabitants of this world have lived with this event as long as Katniss can remember.

Within this predictable event, this year something happens that has never happened before for Katniss: she is affected personally. Her sister Primrose is chosen to compete in the deadly games. Katniss cannot ignore the outcome. That change, that moment where Katniss's own life will be impacted differently than all the previous times, is her Call.

That is what the Call usually brings to the Hero's world: a change. Be it large or small. Whether it is an Invitation or a Mandate, the world that the Hero was used to is faced with something different, and that impact is irreversible. Even if the Hero chooses not to accept the Call (which we will discuss more in depth in Chapter 10), they can't forget that they received it. That knowledge will remain with them and affect them, no matter how they might wish to ignore it. For Katniss, she volunteers to go to the Hunger Games (answering her Invitation) because it is the only way to save her sister.

Before You Move On:

What Calls can you think of from your favorite stories? Can you tell if they were Invitations or Mandates? What changes did the Call bring to the Hero's life?

REAL-WORLD JOURNEYS

When Mahatma Gandhi stepped onto a boat in April of 1893, he was heading toward South Africa for a job. After graduating with a law degree from the prestigious Inner Temple in London, Gandhi had returned to India to begin practicing law. A few years later all he had to show was a failed law practice and a run-in with a British officer that directly affected his livelihood. Everything that he had thought his life was going to be, the things he had worked hard for, was crumbling before his eyes.

Two years after receiving his law degree, as work became scarce, he was approached by a merchant named Dada Abdullah who was in need of assistance. The merchant, owner of a successful shipping business in South Africa, had a distant cousin that was in need of a lawyer. Abdullah offered Gandhi a job that would take him to South Africa for a year. Gandhi, seeing little more than the need for a job, accepted Abdullah's offer and made his way by ship to the other side of the world.

Once he arrived, however, Gandhi's life was drastically altered. He had spent years working to adopt English practices and customs while living in England and had no notion that life in South Africa would be any different. However, from the moment he stepped off the boat he found himself treated in ways he had never anticipated.

Discriminated against for the color of his skin and his Indian heritage, he found himself treated as subhuman. From not being allowed to sit with white people, to being beaten, even being thrown off a train, Gandhi was shown the stark and brutal truth of discrimination that his fellow Indians were experiencing every day.

This experience changed Gandhi permanently. He felt drawn to those who were treated so poorly. He was compelled to do something for those who were suffering under the hands of people who seemed to draw pleasure from their inhumane acts. His eyes were opened. Having witnessed the suffering that was happening all around him, he could not return to his previous ignorance. Gandhi's world had changed, and it was left to him to decide whether he would answer the Call that seemed directed just to him.

When looking for Calls in literature, it is often easy to boil it down to a single event. In our own experiences, it can be a much longer road—a series of seemingly unrelated events, or even just an inner desire for change that can be the beginning of a Journey.

For us, going about living our everyday lives, it can be tempting to think that we do not get obvious messages from the universe about what we should do with our lives. What is more likely is that we are getting messages all the time—we just don't know how to recognize them.

There will be times in our lives when we receive a blatant, clear Call.

Whether these are Invitations or Mandates, we can see that we are being invited towards change. If we are receiving these types of Calls, the best thing we can do is to recognize it for what it is and to answer.

For Gandhi, there was no way to "unsee" the plight of his fellow Indians once he had been exposed to it. He could not ignore their pain and their suffering. The more he listened to this Call, the more he saw what needed to be changed. The more he saw, the more he felt Called to act. He may not have always known the end of the path, but he knew where the path was.

It is also important, though, to learn to look for Calls that are more quiet and subtle. A friend of mine, after talking over these ideas with her, mentioned to me that she had been thinking a lot about getting back into drawing. This was something that she had enjoyed, something she was good at, but hadn't done for a long time. For some reason, in the recent past, she had started thinking about doing it again. The thought was persistent, and she felt a desire to do something when she thought about it.

I believe that this was a Call that she was receiving. Often our Calls seem to come from inside of us. The great news is that we don't have to look far and wide for our Calls. The bad news is that these internal Calls, because we hear them inside of us, can be the easiest to dismiss.

THE CALLS INSIDE OF US

Learning to trust our inner wisdom, to heed the invitations that are coming our way and act upon them, is a Journey in and of itself. We easily dismiss thoughts or feelings as just that: a thought or feeling. Nothing more. Because they exist strictly inside of us, we can brush them aside as meaningless or insubstantial.

To add insult to injury, often, when we actually do act on these ideas or thoughts, the result is disappointing. We felt an impulse to call and

"The only way to get past Resistance is to do the very thing Resistance is telling us not to do."

check on someone, only to find out that they are fine. We apply for a job and don't even get an interview. We can feel like we were mistaken, like we made up the existence of the Invitation and weren't really being nudged by some greater force. The danger here is that we start rejecting Calls because we second-guess ourselves.

ENTER RESISTANCE

From the moment we are presented with a Call to start on a Journey, we are open to experiencing what Steven Pressfield, in his book *The War of Art*, refers to as "Resistance." This is a much larger topic than can be covered here but let me give just a brief overview.

Resistance is the force that acts in opposition to change and improvement. If we imagine Destiny/the Universe/God as the angel on our shoulder urging us toward improvement, Resistance is the red-clad devil arguing for stagnation. Wherever the opportunity for change and growth is present, so too is the desire to avoid that change.

Resistance can take whatever form is necessary to convince us to stay right where we are. Whether it is a physical sensation, a mental script that we run through, or emotional turmoil, Resistance is adept at knowing exactly what to do or say to get us to second-guess and, ultimately, refuse our Call. Any actions that we take that would improve us or the world around us seem to threaten Resistance's very existence. Because of this, you can be sure it is all-out war each and every time change may be on the horizon.

The only way to get past Resistance is to do the very thing Resistance is telling us not to do. We have to learn to read Resistance's tells, because in its very messages lie its weakness. Once we can recognize for ourselves what Resistance looks like in our lives, we can learn to read the signs for how to get rid of it. Wherever Resistance appears, that is where we need to push forward.

GIFTED HANDS

Neurosurgeon Ben Carson speaks of a moment of second-guessing when he was in his clinical year at the University of Michigan's School of Medicine. While watching his instructor struggle to find the foramen ovale (the hole at the base of the skull) on the patient he was operating on, Carson felt strongly that there must be an easier way than the one he was witnessing. He did not know how he knew, but he felt sure there had to be a better way. He recounts:

> Then I started to argue with myself. "You're new at neurosurgery, but you already think you know everything, huh? Remember, Ben, these guys have been doing this kind of surgery for years."
>
> "Yeah," answered another inner voice, "but that doesn't mean they know everything."
>
> "Just leave it alone. One day you'll get your chance to change the world."
> I would have stopped arguing with myself except I couldn't get away from thinking that there must be an easier way. Having to probe for the foramen ovale wasted precious surgery time and it didn't help the patient either.
> "Ok, smart man. Find it then."
> And that's just what I decided to do.
> (Gifted Hands, p. 108)

As simple as it may sound, this is an example of a Call. It all happened inside his mind. The idea that there must be another solution, the Invitation to find it, the immediate Resistance in the form of the "who do you think you are?" script, and finally accepting the Call happened silently and seemingly quite quickly. To the outside observer, nothing had changed at all.

For Ben, however, he felt pulled toward doing something about this surgical situation. Once the gauntlet had been thrown, he had to choose whether or not to pick it up. In this case, he chose to answer the Call and started on a path that improved surgical processes for thousands of doctors. That only happened after he addressed his self-doubt and uncertainty. He had to face his Resistance first and did so by doing the exact thing Resistance was telling him not to do.

CONDITIONAL ACCEPTANCE

The Calls that we receive are part of a larger process intended to help us move forward. Unfortunately for us, we rarely know what the final destination is when we accept a Call. We sometimes create for ourselves what we would consider "acceptable outcomes," and use those projections to determine whether or not we will accept the Call. This occurs even if our projections are not even close to what the ultimate outcome would actually be. We want to know that things will turn out the way we want them to, and rage against the universe when they don't.

The more we trap ourselves in frustration because experiences and events are not the way we think they should be, the more unable we are to have the experiences that we actually need to have.

The same problem occurs when we spend too much emotional energy on the past or the future. Accepting who we are and our situation—as it is, right now—means that we have to avoid dwelling in the past or trying to live in the future. The Calls we are receiving are meant for the person we are today. If we are listening with past- or future-focused ears, those Calls are going unheeded.

THE INEVITABLIITY OF CHANGE

Looking at the way life works, changes come our way whether we desire them or not. We don't get to choose what the Call is, nor where it comes from. We only get to choose whether we accept the Call or not. This can be an intensely frustrating reality, particularly if we picture our life turning out a certain way, or feel like we deserve certain experiences or opportunities, and neither happens.

Remembering that there is something bigger out there, that the path to becoming the best version of ourselves is rarely under our control (because Resistance would encourage us to choose NOT to change), we should start looking for the opportunity in these changes, especially those that come unbidden. Of course, we can choose to be angry about the changes, or allow ourselves to be victims, or even refuse to answer. In the end, fighting our current reality is not only pointless, it can keep us from moving forward.

DESIRE ≠ CALL

One final note about this part of the process: a desire to do something does not automatically make it a Call. There are plenty of people that want to do things that are destructive and harmful to themselves or others; this is *never* the intended purpose of these Journeys. Since Calls come from an outside source (Fate, Destiny, God, Nature, or whatever word you prefer to use), the core of the Journey is moral in nature.

Journey Calls come as a mechanism for individual improvement and contribution, not for wanton violence, needless destruction, or selfishness. While we may have a desire or feel a pull toward these negative behaviors, they are not Calls. As we strive to identify the Calls that we are receiving, we should give heed to those that push us toward virtue, compassion, creation, contribution, and other beneficial behaviors.

Before You Move On:

Thinking about the Calls in your life, consider the specific forms that Calls can take:

- A direct invitation to do something
- Opportunities to learn something new
- Frequent or recurring desires to start (or stop) doing something
- Regular experiences that demonstrate a gap between who you are and who you could be. This can be on the job, in your relationships, etc.

Write down the ideas that come to mind. Don't feel the need to resolve any of the issues, just work on being able to recognize the patterns or characteristics. If you can, include how long/how often the Calls have been coming, as well as any thoughts or emotions that consistently accompany them.

Take some time to write about your experience with Calls, either past or present.

- What form did your Call take?
- Was it an Invitation or a Mandate?
- How did you feel about the Call? Eager to accept?
- Did you refuse the Call before you finally accepted?

3. THE FARTHEST AWAY FROM HOME
I'VE EVER BEEN

The ferry-boat moved slowly across the water. The Buckland shore drew nearer. Sam was the only member of the party who had not been over the river before. He had a strange feeling as the slow gurgling stream slipped by: his old life lay behind in the mists, dark adventure lay in front. He scratched his head, and for a moment had a passing wish that Mr. Frodo could have gone on living quietly at Bag End.

—*The Fellowship of the Ring*, by J.R.R. Tolkien

The decision to accept the Call means that the Hero is going to have to enter the unfamiliar world of their Journey, and that means leaving home. Progress can only happen if they are willing to leave what they know, what they are comfortable with, and enter into the unknown. Standing between the Hero and the world they need to enter is a line that the Hero needs to cross called the **Threshold**. Much like the threshold of a door, the Threshold represents taking a step from one world and entering into another.

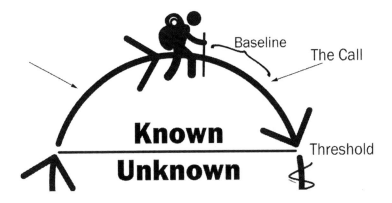

If the Hero is physically going somewhere, the crossing takes place in a physical space. It may be as drastic as traveling to a new world, or as simple as walking across the street. The act of physically moving to a new location is a powerful one, and the change is immediate.

Other Thresholds occur in more figurative or symbolic spheres. Crossing the Threshold will occur any time the Hero is moving from the known to the unknown, and can be mental, emotional, spiritual, or all of the above. For example, a character who loses a loved one moves from the world where their loved was present (the "Known") to the world where their loved one is gone (the "Unknown").

The same can be said for a character presented with a truth that alters the way they see the world, a change in financial status, or a role change in their society. As long as the Hero is being taken from what they know to what they don't know, they are crossing a Threshold.

SAMWISE GAMGEE: RELUCTANT HERO

One of my favorite moments to demonstrate this Threshold crossing comes from J.R.R. Tolkien's *The Fellowship of the Ring*. Following a long-planned departure from the Shire to carry the One Ring to safety, Frodo, Sam, and Pippin have traveled many miles from their home in Hobbiton. They have already experienced something odd in their travels: a stranger, dressed in black, riding a black horse, seeking out "Frodo Baggins." Though well within the geographic bounds they are familiar with, this new player alters their feelings of safety.

There is a brief moment (as mentioned in the beginning of this chapter) when, once they've joined up with Merry and are riding the ferry toward Buckland, we get insight into Samwise's experience of crossing a Threshold.

In this short but important moment, we learn that Sam has never been over the river before, and as he sits in the boat he is crossing a physical Threshold. But, it also gives us a glimpse into the emotional impact the crossing has on Sam. He feels this crossing as a turning point in his life. He senses that his "old life" is over, knowing that the "dark adventure" ahead of them will change not just him, but Frodo as well.

While Peter Jackson's movie interpretation of Sam crossing the Threshold does not occur in the same way as Tolkien's book, he also allows Sam a moment to reflect on the importance of this crossing. In this case, Frodo and Sam are starting the adventure alone, and as they walk through an ordinary field of grass, Sam stops dead in his tracks.

"This is it," Sam announces.

"This is what?" Frodo asks, turning to look at him.

"If I take one more step, this is the farthest away from home I've ever been."

Frodo takes a few steps back toward him. "Come on, Sam," he says.

Sam hesitates, looking at the actual point on the ground that represents this crossing, then finally takes a slow step forward.

This is a quick, quiet moment in an otherwise intense and fast-paced story, but its importance should not be overlooked. Characters who step over the Threshold do so without having any idea of what they are getting into—even if they think they know. That they would hesitate or have a fleeting wish that things could somehow be different, is an indication of what crossing the Threshold means.

THRESHOLD GUARDIANS

In some stories, when the character is ready to cross the Threshold they come face to face with an obstacle that blocks their way. Some Heroes, in their eagerness to find change, attempt to leave the Known World before they are actually ready. If they were to cross the Threshold and enter the Unknown World, it would be destructive, much more than the Hero can handle.

In these cases, a Threshold Guardian stands at that crucial crossing point and prevents the Hero from making that step before they are truly ready. These guardians can be kind or foreboding, familiar or foreign, but the message is the same: "You aren't ready yet." A guardian who does their job correctly stands at the Threshold, turning the Hero back, time and time again if necessary, until the Hero has reached the point where they are ready to progress. At that moment, the Threshold Guardian steps aside and allows the Hero to pass into the unknown.

In literature, these guardian characters are often adults in the lives of younger characters. The younger characters frequently have a great desire to "get out" or "escape" the boring world of home, but often their desire to leave home does not match their ability to survive away from it.

In this case, they may have a parent or other family member or a teacher that reminds them that they are not ready. This can create tension between the characters, particularly if this exchange happens frequently and is only resolved when the Hero is actually ready.

Guardians are not always for younger characters, however. Samurai Jack, the titular character of Genndy Tartakovsky's animated series, encounters a character that shows how Threshold Guardians can still appear for characters who are capable, even powerful in many ways, but perhaps not prepared for this specific Journey.

While facing his nemesis, the evil wizard Aku, Jack gets magically thrust into the future where Aku has taken over the world and shaped it to his own evil desires. Jack travels the land, desperately trying to find a way back to the past so that he can stop this terrible future from becoming a reality.

In episode XXXII (titled "Jack and the Traveling Creatures"), Jack learns of a portal that will take him back to his time. There is only one problem: standing in Jack's way is a character who is (appropriately) named "The Guardian." Jack asks the Guardian to step aside, as he has no desire to fight him. The Guardian explains that his job, his only job, is to guard this portal. The only way through is to defeat the Guardian.

> *"For countless eons I have guarded this magical power of time travel. All have been denied, from the mightiest of giants, to the tiniest of warriors. You see, Samurai, only one man has been prophesized (sic) to defeat me. And that man is the only man who can use this time passage. And you, my man... ain't that man."*

The fight that ensues is epic, and Jack ultimately fails to defeat the Guardian. In defeat, Jack is taken away from the portal by a dragon. Once he is gone, the portal shows to the Guardian the man who is to ultimately defeat him. In this case, that man is an older version of Jack—the person Jack is meant to become.

While it seems strange that the Guardian would say that Jack isn't the one who would defeat him, in this case, it is the *current* version of Jack that is unable to win the battle. Until Jack is strong enough and skilled enough to beat the Guardian, he will not be able to overcome the obstacles that await on the other side of the portal. He needs to grow first, change, improve, and then he can cross the Threshold that waits for him.

"Our brains hate uncertainty, literally perceiving it in the same way that we perceive threats."

Thresholds, and Threshold Guardians, serve a very important purpose in the Hero's story, though they often don't get a lot of attention or fanfare. Whether the Threshold is internal or external, "crossing over" marks the beginning of big changes for the Hero, regardless of the size of their individual Journey.

Before You Move On:

What Thresholds can you identify in your favorite stories? Is there a physical crossing? A symbolic crossing? Does the character have a Threshold Guardian? Do they pause before crossing, or march ahead boldly? What does the crossing represent for the Hero?

REAL-WORLD JOURNEYS

In April 2007, Ariana Huffington, co-founder and editor-in-chief of the Huffington Post, opened her eyes to find herself lying on the floor of her office in a pool of blood. She later found that she had passed out and hit her desk on the way down, cutting her eye and breaking her cheekbone.

This incident began a series of doctors' appointments, MRI's, CAT scans, and echocardiograms as they struggled to determine the cause of the collapse. In the end, the truth was almost harder to accept than some underlying medical condition: she passed out due to lack of sleep and exhaustion.

For the first time in her career, everything she had been taught about being successful—working excessive hours, saying "yes" as often as possible, never taking a break—failed her. The success she had experienced in the fast-moving, cutthroat world of the news was, quite suddenly, not worth the cost.

As she saw it, the accident was a wake-up call that she finally heeded. What lay before her was a quest to answer the question: Was this the life she wanted?

In our lives, we have just as many examples of Thresholds as you will find in literature. Regardless of whether we like it or not, change and growth only come as we leave our comfort zone and push ourselves to learn from, or deal with, something new. At school, at work, in relationships, in pursuing interests, pretty much any situation where change is a factor, Thresholds must be crossed.

DEALING WITH UNCERTAINTY

Crossing Thresholds is akin to taking a step into the darkness. We literally have no way to fully understand what is on the other side of that line. Uncertainty can be difficult to deal with.

Our brains hate uncertainty, literally perceiving it in the same way that we perceive threats. We experience physical and emotional reactions when dealing with uncertainty, and they aren't all pretty.

Hesitation at the point of crossing is normal, and we should not berate ourselves should we find ourselves concerned about the path that lies ahead. If there weren't questions or uncertainty, it wouldn't be a true Threshold.

Understanding that this hesitation is normal is important, because these feelings are not necessarily warnings to turn back. If what you are feeling is a reasonable amount of trepidation, that feeling may actually be a sign that you are right where you are supposed to be.

NOT ALWAYS LINES IN THE SAND

Don't forget that Thresholds don't have to be a physical line that we step over. Any time we are thrust into a situation or an experience where we don't know what we are doing, we have crossed a Threshold. Young adults who have to take care of their own finances for the first time are crossing a Threshold. Experiencing the passing of a parent or loved one is crossing a Threshold.

Whether obvious or subtle, the key to recognizing a Threshold is recognizing your level of knowledge and comfort on the other side of the line. Crossing from the Known to the Unknown is literally that: if we are already prepared for what is to come, we are not crossing a Threshold. We are at a different point within the Journey.

For Ariana Huffington, stepping into the Unknown meant leaving the world where logic, drive, and business savvy had been the solution for any problem. None of those were sufficient to solve the problems she now had to face. Instead, she had to turn to solutions of a spiritual nature, solutions that in her Known World were ignored, dismissed, or even mocked. Stepping into this Unknown World went against everything she had believed up to that point, requiring an openness to ideas and practices that were foreign to her.

I'm a firm believer in the power of having the right word for things. Knowing how to talk about that experience of stepping into the darkness, knowing what it means to cross over those lines, goes a long way toward helping us to accept, and maybe even embrace, what is happening.

THE THRESHOLD GUARDIAN NEXT DOOR

Just as in literature, Threshold Guardians are a part of our Journeys as well. These can be a boss, a teacher, even a parent or friend. The job of the Guardian is the same in our lives: to keep us from crossing Thresholds that we are not ready to cross.

One of the great difficulties when dealing with Threshold Guardians in real life is knowing the difference between a Guardian and a nay-sayer. As we are starting to move toward change, we can feel pushback from a variety of sources. This includes people around us who, even with the best of intentions, warn us away from the path we are on.

The difference between a Guardian and a nay-sayer has to do with perspective. Guardians have perspective enough to be able to see not only the truth about who we are and what we are capable of, but also what will be required on the other side of the Threshold. Their message is a hopeful one: we may not be ready yet, but we can be if we continue to prepare. That may be difficult to hear, but when spoken from a place of perspective we can see the truth in what they say.

Nay-sayers, on the other hand, speak out of fear. They may be uncomfortable with the potential changes that they see because they themselves are afraid. Again, their intentions may be good, but unless they are speaking from a place of perspective and not a place of fear, they are not helping us on our Journey.

Before You Move On

Take some time to think back to experiences that could be considered crossing a Threshold. How did you feel at the time? What was the experience like? Was there a Guardian? If so, what did you have to do before you were ready to cross?

Take some time to write in your journal about your Thresholds. Consider the following questions:

- Define the Known/Unknown for your crossing.
- Was it a physical, mental, emotional, symbolic crossing?
- Or perhaps it was more than one?
- How did you handle stepping into the Unknown?
- Did you have a Threshold Guardian? What did they tell you?

---

4. BRACE FOR IMPACT

"Welcome," said Hagrid, "to Diagon Alley."

He grinned at Harry's amazement. They stepped through the archway. Harry looked quickly over his shoulder and saw the archway shrink instantly back into solid wall...Harry wished he had about eight more eyes. He turned his head in every direction as they walked up the street, trying to look at everything at once..."

—*Harry Potter and the Sorcerer's Stone* by JK Rowling

Stepping across the Threshold is a momentous task. For many characters, this is their first venture into an Unknown World, particularly one of this level of importance. Doing so may have required all the courage and effort the Hero could muster, and they often cross the Threshold hoping that the rest of the Journey will be easy. They are in for an unpleasant surprise.

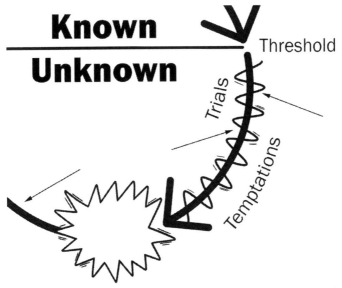

Crossing the Threshold means entering the Unknown, starting on a series of **Trials**. The disparity between what the Hero was capable of before and what is required of them now is striking. They are completely out of their element. Just about everything they try to do results in failure. They try to communicate, but they don't speak the language. They try to make a purchase, but don't understand the economic system. They try to cast a spell, but don't understand magic. Even tasks that resemble something the Hero is actually capable of doing are, to some degree, different enough to result in failure. These ups and downs, attempts and failures, can feel like getting kicked while you are down: there is almost no way to catch a break.

This series of Trials is not meant to be devastating but can certainly feel that way. Contrary to what the Hero may believe, these Trials are not even unique to the Hero. They are simply the reality of stepping into an Unknown World.

TEMPTATION TO QUIT EARLY

The difficulty of being at such a disadvantage can often cause the character to experience the single most seductive **Temptation** of the entire Journey: the Temptation to quit and return home before the

Journey is complete.

Some characters develop a form of amnesia, forgetting their unhappiness and discontent at home and potentially convincing themselves that things weren't really all that bad. Maybe they tell themselves they had just been exaggerating, or that they just misunderstood certain people or situations. Compared to the harsh reality of what they are facing, their memories of home become fluid, and even deceptive.

Without evidence to the contrary, the Hero may convince themselves that being home is better than being pushed and challenged in such difficult ways. The Temptation to abandon the Journey is very real during this phase, and the consequences for doing so are just as real.

DIAGON ALLEY

Harry Potter provides a great example of a character who gets hit pretty hard by the gap between what he knows (the "Muggle" world) and what he does not know (the Wizarding world). After receiving a letter from Hogwarts School of Witchcraft and Wizardry, Harry knows two things: first, he is a wizard. Second, he is expected to be at wizarding school for the coming school year. Since Harry's Threshold Guardian (his Uncle Vernon) refuses to step aside and allow Harry to begin his Journey, the headmaster of Hogwarts sends Hagrid (a powerful and rather intimidating giant) to see that Harry is able to begin.

Since Harry had no idea that wizards existed, the knowledge that he *is* one sees him crossing over an internal Threshold. Physically leaving home to head to a place he had never heard of sees him crossing an external Threshold. In both cases, Harry clearly has no idea what he is doing.

"These experiences, exasperating as they may be, do have a cumulative effect on the Hero: progress."

Consider the first place Harry is taken by his escort Hagrid: Diagon Alley. For centuries Diagon Alley has served as a shopping area for the wizard world, where students of Hogwarts visit to gather the necessary supplies for the coming school year.

Armed with the list for First Years, Hagrid leads Harry down the street to find specific shops where Harry can purchase things like uniforms, books, wands, and cauldrons. It is very apparent that Harry knows absolutely nothing about this process. He knows nothing about money in this world, including how to withdraw it from the bank. He is asked numerous questions to which he does not know the answer. He is introduced to food that is completely foreign. Without Hagrid's help, Harry would have been unable to function.

Gaining knowledge of Diagon Alley is only the beginning, however. Harry has to actually get to Hogwarts, which requires boarding a train at Platform 9 3/4—a task Harry has no idea how to complete on his own. Once at Hogwarts, he is introduced to courses, teachers, rituals, and social classes that did not exist in his previous world, and that he must now learn how to maneuver. To complicate things even more, it seems that the school itself is under attack, and the unknown danger is affecting everyone. Harry is surrounded by a world that is completely foreign, even though it exists in tandem with what he knew before. The transition is difficult and fraught with frustrations and missteps.

These experiences, exasperating as they may be, do have a cumulative effect on the Hero: progress. Each experience, if learned from, means becoming a little bit more capable. Slowly—often more slowly than the Hero would like—they find ways to handle this Unknown World. In fact, this is exactly how they become stronger, faster, smarter, wiser, or whatever else is needed. The steps are incremental and come with seemingly built-in failures that must be endured. But, if the Hero is willing, they can overcome both the Trials and the Temptation to quit the Journey early.

> **Before You Move On**
>
> The Trials and Temptations part of the Hero's story is often the longest. We travel with the Hero through these difficulties, watching them grow, seeing them progress. What examples of Trials can you identify? Did they experience the Temptation to quit the Journey? How did they handle the Trials and Temptation?

REAL-WORLD JOURNEYS

On March 4, 1861, Abraham Lincoln stepped forward at the Capitol to give his first inaugural address. Overshadowed by the threat of a civil war, Lincoln's words to those who saw him as an enemy were heartfelt and intended to mend the divided nation. The final words of his speech expressed this desire:

> *"I am loath to close. We are not enemies, but friends. We must not be enemies. Though passion may have strained it must not break our bonds of affection. The mystic chords of memory, stretching from every battlefield and patriot grave to every living heart and hearthstone all over this broad land, will yet swell the chorus of the Union, when again touched, as surely they will be, by the better angels of our nature."*

The path that led Abraham Lincoln to the White House was far from easy. From an early life full of tragedy and loss, he learned early that anything he wanted he was going to have to fight for. A glance at a timeline of his life demonstrates this:

1818 His mother died.
1831 Failed in business.
1832 Ran for state legislature - lost.
1834 Ran for state legislature again - won.
1835 Was engaged to be married, sweetheart died and his heart was broken.
1836 Had a total nervous breakdown and was in bed for six months.
1838 Sought to become speaker of the state legislature - defeated.
1840 Sought to become elector - defeated.
1843 Ran for Congress - lost.
1846 Ran for Congress again - this time he won - went to Washington

1848 Ran for re-election to Congress - lost.
1849 Sought the job of land officer in his home state - rejected.
1854 Ran for Senate of the United States - lost.
1856 Sought the vice-presidential nomination at his party's national convention - got less than 100 votes.
1858 Ran for U.S. Senate again - again he lost.
1860 Elected president of the United States.

The man who stood before the nation on that March day had been forged in the furnace of experience, knowing both success and failure, joy and despair.

For all of the courage that it may have taken to answer the Call and step across the Threshold, it really is only the beginning of what is to come. Our expectations about how the world works, how the process of change works, are most often in direct conflict with what actually needs to happen for us to grow. This step in the process is one of the most misunderstood, and because of that, can cause the most turmoil.

GROWTH MINDSET

Navigating this section of the Journey, particularly the Temptation to quit and return home prematurely, requires a particular way of looking at the world. In the words of Carol Dweck, author of *Mindset: The New Psychology of Success*, we need to move away from a "fixed mindset"— where we believe we are unable to learn and change—to a "growth mindset."

If our mindset is fixed, any failure we experience becomes evidence that we just don't have what it takes, and we never will. With a growth mindset, on the other hand, each attempt we make adds to our vast library of experience, which we can learn from and improve upon. The Journey process itself is a testament to the fact that we can change and grow if we let the experience guide us where we need to go.

PLAN TO FAIL

Tell me if this sounds familiar (for either yourself or someone you know): after feeling like you needed to make a change for a long time, you finally decide that the moment has arrived. You are going to do it. You are going to take the plunge.

If you are anything like me, you make a bunch of plans, schedules, and lists. You buy all the appropriate tools or supplies. You are excited, and just know that this time change is really going to happen.

For most people, the happy feelings end as soon as you actually start acting on those plans. As you start to make the changes, you find that your plans were painfully unrealistic. The path becomes quickly rocky, painful, and disappointing. The way things are "supposed" to work is nothing like your experience. You force yourself to keep going and going, but at some point, you slip up, and slipping up means you are a failure. You return back to your normal routine, berating yourself for being weak, promising yourself that the next time will be different.

If this has happened to you, please know you are not alone. Failure is an integral and crucial part of the learning process, despite the messages we receive from society at large. Learning to see failure as a teacher—as feedback instead of a terminal state--changes our experience dramatically.

We are bombarded each and every day with promises of quick results, of rapid improvement, of immediate changes. While these claims may be able to produce results, the results are rarely sustainable. The programs and promises are trying to jump ahead in the process, without creating the actual changes that would be needed to sustain those improvements in the long-run.

What happens more often than not is that we accept the Call and want to believe that is all it takes. It is like thinking: I want to change;

therefore, I have changed. We try to skip to the end of the process without paying the price.

THE UGLY TRUTH ABOUT CHANGE

For lasting change to occur, accepting the Call is the very first step in a series of steps—all of which are going to be difficult in some way and to some degree. Many of these steps will include failure. Smooth sailing, if it ever happens, comes at the end of a long, difficult road.

This happens not just with people trying to change their health habits or wanting to be more productive at work or any of a number of desired changes. Parents decide they want to change the way they are relating with their child, only to find the strategy they read about doesn't work the way they thought it would. An employer wants to change the way business is done, but finds resistance in the ranks, even when the change is important or even necessary. Deciding to change is a crucial step—even a difficult step—but it is not the last step.

I realize that this can sound like a picture of gloom and doom, but it doesn't have to be. Knowing what the change process looks like alters our understanding of struggle and failure and can be very empowering. Struggle means building strength, patience, perseverance, understanding, and more. Failure no longer means we are broken, or we'll never be enough, or that we made the wrong decision; it is simply part of the process of change.

As long as we are learning with every attempt, we will get better. As long as we don't give in to the Temptation to quit, the Trials will be meaningful. Just as Lincoln's road to the White House was full of difficulty and failure, those experiences shaped and changed him. They allowed him to have patience, empathy, courage, and perspective. All of these qualities were crucial to what the Journey was preparing him for, even if those changes came at great difficulty.

Ultimately, the Trials and Temptation phase of the Journey takes up the bulk of the time. It may take more time than we want. In fact, it usually does. But if navigated correctly, we will go from being a novice to being competent. Knowledge and skills do not come cheap, but the price we pay is absolutely worth it.

Remember: the struggle is the point. We question whether change is worth it. We question if our pathway is sound or will really lead to change. Without putting strain on our muscles, without pushing them past what they are used to doing, we cannot become stronger. This is true in almost every facet of our lives. Struggle, done correctly, builds us up more powerfully than any other method. We may be able to cheat the system temporarily, but for long-term change there are no shortcuts.

Before You Move On:

Take some time to think about the Trials you experienced on the path toward change. Take some time to write and reflect about these experiences.

- What experiences might you have had that were frustrating or difficult?
- In what ways might you have experienced failure? How did you deal with it?
- What was the progression of your experiences? (In other words, how might your experiences have built upon each other?)

5. A LITTLE HELP FROM MY FRIENDS

Use the Force Luke.

Let go, Luke.

Luke, trust me.

—Obi Wan Kenobi, *Star Wars IV: A New Hope* by George Lucas

Amidst the onslaught of the Trials and Temptations phase, the Hero becomes acutely aware of everything they don't know. The gap between who they are and what they can do, and who they need to be and what they need to do, is enormous. This disparity would be overwhelming and, ultimately, too much for the Hero to handle.

Fortunately, the Journey supplies a solution for the Hero to help them through the difficult time: *Helpers* and *Mentors*. Helpers and Mentors can enter the story of the Hero at any time. They may be there from the beginning, join the Hero once crossing the Threshold, or show up right before the end. The placement of their entrance is unimportant. What matters is what the Helpers and Mentors do within the context of the Journey.

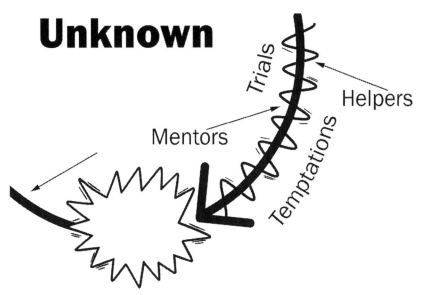

Both of these types of characters act as a support to the Hero, but their roles are very distinct.

HELPERS

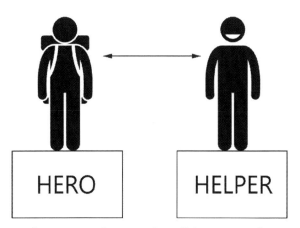

Helpers are characters who are, for all intents and purposes, on the same level as the Hero. They are often the same age, though they do not have to be. More importantly, they have skill sets and knowledge that the Hero lacks, allowing them to fill in the Hero's gaps at crucial moments. The Hero can't find their next class? The Helper knows the way. The Hero doesn't know where to send the monthly reports? The Helper lends a hand. Getting through the day-to-day tasks of the Unknown is where the Helper really shines, and their influence is both specific and necessary.

However, Helpers are also, in some ways, dependent upon the Hero. The Hero/Helper relationships are often reciprocal, with the Hero and Helpers working together to overcome the most immediate and pressing challenges, offering friendship as well as support.

ESCAPE FROM THE DEATH STAR

This balance of characters makes for some very memorable friendships as well as adventures. Escaping from the Death Star in *Star Wars Episode IV: A New Hope* would have been impossible for Luke Skywalker to accomplish on his own. Starting with the very first encounter after their ship has been pulled into the moon-sized space station, it is the fact that Han Solo is not just a pilot, but is also a smuggler, that allows their small group to avoid detection.

As they progress, each member of the group is needed for different tasks. Luke comes up with the idea of how to get to the detention level to rescue Princess Leia, but it is the now-rescued princess that gets them out of the next mess by shooting a path into the trash compactor. Once in the trash compactor, Luke's trusted droid R2-D2 rescues them all.

Between Luke, Han, Leia, and the droids, they have the knowledge and skills necessary to escape the Death Star. Individually, they would have failed. This pattern can be traced through the rest of the movies, and even into the sequels. The point is that the Hero cannot do these things on their own.

NO PREREQUISITES

Helpers do not have to be human (or the same species) as the Hero. In fact, they don't even have to be alive. Tom Hanks' character Chuck Noland in *Castaway* is literally by himself on an island in the middle of the ocean. You would think that he would be an example of a Hero without a Helper. Those who have seen the movie, however, know how crucial to his survival Wilson—the volleyball—is. Chuck has enough knowledge to survive the initial few days on the island and is able to develop the skills he needs for long-term survival. The help he needs is emotional help; he needs companionship. Without any form of connection, it is possible that he would not have survived the island.

Helpers can even be memories of someone that the Hero cares about. The knowledge that there is someone waiting at home for them can act as a support in difficult times, even if that person is not physically present. Helpers can also be characters who act as antagonists to the Hero, showing the Hero what they don't want to be or do. It would be impossible to list all of the ways Helpers can function. More important is the ability to recognize those entities that fill in gaps for the Hero, allowing them to progress through their Trials and Temptations.

The Helper characters can be with the Hero from the very beginning of the story to the very end because of the reciprocal nature of their relationship. Just as the Hero grows, the Helpers also grow. Many of them go through their own Journey cycle right along with the Hero. As they grow individually, their ability to impact each other's stories also grows.

MENTORS

Mentors, on the other hand, are functioning at a completely different level than the Hero. Not every story has one, at least not one that actively functions in the story. If there is a Mentor, they are obvious. Life experience has given them one crucial thing that the Hero (or the Helpers) doesn't have: perspective.

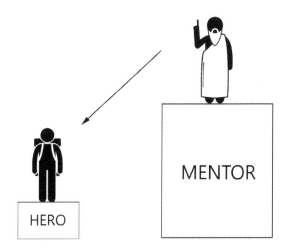

Mentor characters usually know the big picture. They know the major players. They know the history of the situation or the conflict. Because of this unique perspective, Mentors are usually only minimally interested in the immediate crisis facing the Hero. Instead, they focus on preparing the Hero for the larger goals that the Journey is leading them toward. This larger perspective can sometimes lead to the Mentor seeming distant, disconnected, or even strange. Their wisdom, however, is always crucial for the Hero at some point during the Journey.

Harry Potter describes this well when he says,

> *"He's a funny man, Dumbledore. I think he sort of wanted to give me a chance. I think he knows more or less everything that goes on here, you know. I reckon he had a pretty good idea we were going to try, and instead of stopping us, he just taught us enough to help."*

> *(Harry Potter and the Sorcerer's Stone, p 201)*

HELP ME, OBI WAN KENOBI

Continuing with Star Wars as our example, Obi Wan Kenobi is clearly a Mentor character for Luke. As a character, he knows all about the history not only of the Empire and the Rebellion, but also of Luke's father. Obi Wan acts as a teacher when it comes to Luke learning to use the Force—something that is crucial since the Jedi were almost completely wiped out.

In the short time that he has with Luke, Obi Wan has a life-changing impact on him. He shows Luke that there is truth to the stories that Luke grew up with and puts him firmly on the path to discovering his true calling: to become a Jedi and defeat Darth Vader.

Without Obi Wan specifically, Luke's life would have been vastly different. Without a knowledge of the Force, without a knowledge of the history of Luke's family, without the perspective to see where Luke really needed to go—as opposed to where Luke *wanted* to go—the fate of the Star Wars universe is bleak.

Comparing the story roles of Han and Leia as opposed to Obi Wan in Luke's Journey hopefully demonstrates the difference between the two roles. Again, they are both important, but in very different ways. There is a similar role comparison with Harry Potter's friends Ron and Hermione as opposed to the headmaster of Hogwarts Dumbledore. Or the Hobbits Samwise, Merry, and Pippin's support of Frodo as opposed to the great wizard Gandalf. These differences allow them to fill in very specific holes for the Hero trying to make their way through the Trials and Temptations.

AS A WARNING

One important note about Mentors (now that we've considered a few examples): Mentors always die. Alright, that might be a bit dramatic, but it is true in a sense—though the death may be more symbolic than literal.

Because of the wisdom and strength of Mentor characters, the Hero often becomes dependent upon them. They turn to the Mentor increasingly for each question and every Trial, relying on the Mentor instead of their own skills or knowledge. Ultimately, without a change, the Hero would cease to progress, relying on the merits of the Mentor to carry them through. Therefore, the Mentor must step out of the picture.

Often in stories, this means the Mentor literally dies, leaving the Hero alone to face the trials ahead. You see this with the three Mentors that I previously mentioned (Obi Wan, Dumbledore, and Gandalf). Their deaths are painful and heart-wrenching for the Hero, and they may feel that there is no way for them to continue without their Mentor. If the Mentor has done their job, however, the Hero has everything they need, everything the Mentor could give them.

If the Mentor does not literally die, they symbolically die. This can happen through stepping back, removing themselves from the situation, or acknowledging to the Hero that they can no longer function as their Mentor.

Rupert Giles, the Watcher for Buffy the Vampire Slayer, comes to this realization in the episode "Once More, with Feeling." He recognizes how Buffy is relying on him in situations where she is fully capable and he has become a crutch that she leans on too often. In the song titled "Standing," Giles sings:

The cries around you
You don't hear at all
'Cause you know I'm here to take that call
So you just lie there when
You should be standing tall.

Recognizing Buffy's reliance on him to do those things she needs to do on her own, he takes the difficult step of leaving Sunnydale, and Buffy, so that she can become who she needs to be. The Hero has to learn to stand on their own two feet; with the Mentor present, that might not happen.

With Helpers and Mentors in place, the Hero is able to make it through the Trials and Temptations. Step by step, experience by experience, they learn a little more, experience a little more, and build the skills that they need to begin to be competent and capable.

Before You Move On:

Think about some of your favorite Helpers and Mentors. What did they contribute to the Hero on their Journey? What would have happened to the Hero without them? What perspective do the Mentors have that the Hero needs? Does the Mentor survive?

REAL-WORLD JOURNEYS

When Chesley "Sully" Sullenberger was 15, he had developed a deep-seated desire to learn how to fly an airplane. Growing up in Texas, he had watched military jets from the Air Force base near his house and had become fascinated by them enough to start studying them on his own.

At 15 his parents arranged for Sully to learn to fly from a local crop-duster who had also spent time teaching pilots in the area. Mr. Cook put Sully in the front seat and sat himself in the back seat with his own set of controls, prepared to take over at any moment as he "followed (Sully) through." The experience was exhilarating.

Over the next few weeks, Sully logged more than seven hours of flight time with Mr. Cook coaching him on the techniques and skills of piloting. One day, things went differently.

Sully recounted that as he flew the regular route, Mr. Cook tapped him on the shoulder:

>*"All right," he said. "Bring it in for a landing and taxi over to the hangar." I did as I was told, and when we got there, he hopped out of the plane. "Ok," he said. "Take it up and land three times by yourself."*

>*He didn't wish me luck. That wasn't his way. I'm not saying he was gruff*

or unfeeling. It's just that he was very matter-of-fact about things. He had obviously decided: The kid's ready. Let him go. He expected I wouldn't fall out of the sky. I'd be OK.

As I flew, it was as if I could hear his voice. Use the rudder to keep the controls coordinated. Even though he wasn't there in the airplane, his words were still with me.

Though I had less than eight hours in the air, Mr. Cook had given me confidence. He had given me permission to discover that I could get a plane safely into the air and safely back to the ground.

(Highest Duty, pp. 9-10)

Focusing separately on "Trials and Temptations" and "Helpers and Mentors" can seem a bit misleading—they are most definitely intertwined. However, it is vital to establish how difficult the Trials and Temptations section of the Journey is, so that the importance of Helpers and Mentors can be truly understood.

Once we have crossed a Threshold, we are in over our head. Plain and simple. If we are not, then chances are good we are in a different part of the Journey process. Crossing the Threshold means being incompetent at functioning within the new world. Without help, the process will be too difficult and take too much time and energy. That is why Helpers and Mentors are so crucial.

As was mentioned, Helpers and Mentors fulfill distinct roles for the Hero in a story. This is no different in real life. The tricky part for us is to make sure we are recognizing and utilizing these resources in the best ways possible.

"*Once we have crossed a Threshold, we are in over our head. Plain and simple.*"

HELPERS

The Helpers in our lives are those people that we turn to when we have immediate needs. This can be the neighbor we call in an emergency, the family member who knows how to fix cars, or the friend who knows just what to say to keep us going.

Much as in literature, these relationships are reciprocal, where you are called upon by them just as frequently. They cheer us up, encourage us, commiserate with us, and otherwise fill in holes where our own abilities and knowledge fall short. Hopefully you have many people in your life that act in this supporting role, and it is just as important to consider where you act as a Helper for others.

With support from the Helpers in our lives, we are able to focus on practicing skills, gaining knowledge, and building our symbolic muscles in preparation for the tasks that are ahead of us. More than just allowing us to get to work, Helpers actually improve the quality of our lives. As Helen Keller said of the friends (or Helpers, as we would call them) in her life,

> *"Thus it is that my friends have made the story of my life. In a thousand ways they have turned my limitations into beautiful privileges, and enabled me to walk serene and happy in the shadow cast by my deprivation"* (The Story of My Life, p 111).

MENTORS

Mentors are those rare people in our lives that seem to always know exactly what to say to get us back on track. They can correct us without our feeling threatened. They can call us out when we need it, and we know inside that what they are saying is true, even if it hurts. We trust their opinion and seek out their guidance.

Whether the Mentor is providing perspective for a specific skill or task we want/need to accomplish, or general help for the larger pictures of life, we know that they have our best interest at heart even if—and especially when—they say things that are hard to hear. Unlike Helpers with whom we spend a great deal of time, Mentors may only act as an occasional presence in our lives. That occasional presence, however, is measured not by the quantity of minutes, but by the quality of the interaction.

What qualities do Mentors possess that set them apart? It would be difficult to put together lists of character traits, as they are just as often grumpy as happy, young as old, friendly as antisocial. More important than character traits are the things the Mentor does to support and challenge.

Greg Daniels, television writer/producer/director, has acted as a Mentor to writer/actress Mindy Kaling since she started working on the television comedy *The Office*. Her description of what Greg has done for her encapsulates it this way:

> *The word mentor is funny because it has a pedagogical, formal feel to it. Greg never sat me down and said, "I believe in you, kid. Now, here, take this antique fountain pen that W.C. Fields gave me and go make something of yourself." He's always just provided opportunities for me, set an example of how to be a leader, invited me to his house for dinner sometimes, and sat in consoling silence across from me when I was going through heartbreak. He's wonderful. (Why Not Me?, p. 87)*

That idea seems to be the key: knowing us well enough to know what we need, when we need it. Mentors open up opportunities for us to grow, supporting us in ways that meet us where we are, and push us forward.

In some cases, Mentors complete their role and may assume the new role of Helper, or just steps out of the role altogether. This is not an easy transition for either party, particularly when it is someone we know well and have a long history together. These issues are certainly not insurmountable. Welcoming the transition can make it easier.

Sometimes identifying Mentors in our lives can be easy. We can access Mentors directly (in person) or indirectly (through books, songs, movies, etc.). There are also times when it may feel like we don't have a specific person in our life to act in this role. Mentors in our world, just like in literary worlds, are not always available, and may come and go from our lives. We may have to seek out a Mentor (possibly a Journey in and of itself), or perhaps just recognize those that are already present in our lives (also a potential Journey). There is no template for Mentors in the real world, nor is there only one way to find them.

Regardless, it is important to remember that without Mentors we would get so caught up in the day-to-day that we would never make it to the larger things we are meant to do.

If you have a Mentor, make sure to take the time to listen. If they are a true Mentor, what they have to say will be vital at some point along the way.

POSITIVE AND NEGATIVE INFLUENCES

Because we are human, none of us is perfect. This holds true not only for the Helpers and Mentors in our lives, but also for ourselves when we act as a Helper or a Mentor to someone else. However, in real-life you see more examples of people acting out their roles in ways that are not always positive.

The role of the Helper is to contribute where their knowledge and skills are needed, support the Hero in the here-and-now, and fit into a larger system of help and support.

If, on the other hand, they try to help outside of the knowledge or skill level, create obstacles instead of helping the Hero to surmount them, or try to create a situation where they are the sole support for the Hero, they stop being a Helper and become a Hindrance.

Some examples of Hindrances would be friends who always ask for help but never give it, family members who isolate the Hero from their other support systems for selfish reasons, fellow students who create problems instead of helping to solve them, or anyone who wants to keep the Hero from progressing because it would adversely affect them.

The role of the Mentor is to contribute their perspective, to help the Hero see past the here-and-now, and to intervene (as opposed to interfere). Intervening happens when the Hero is allowed to act on their own, and the Mentor only steps in if it is clear that the Hero either does not understand the situation correctly or does not have the skills to accomplish the task. If the Mentor did not intervene, the Hero would end up completely off-track. Mentors work best when they get the Hero back on track.

Mentors that do not fulfill their role act as Manipulators. They try to act as a Mentor in areas where they do not have perspective, their vision of the Hero and the Hero's future is tainted by personal interest, they try to skip parts of the process instead of allowing the Hero to experience difficulty, and they interfere (as opposed to intervene). Interfering happens when the Mentor acts in a way to control the outcome, making things happen the way they want, regardless of what is best for the Hero.

Examples of Manipulators would be coaches who value winning over the development of their players, teachers who push personal agendas over student growth, and parents who either push their children into paths (such as being a doctor, lawyer, etc.) for their own bragging rights, or refuse to allow their children to struggle and fail.

There are many more examples of both Hindrances and Manipulators, but the end result is the same: the Hero does not progress. One of the tasks for our Journey may be to learn how to identify these influences in our lives. We then can either work to transform them into the Helpers and Mentors that we need, or to distance ourselves from their obstructive influences. This is a complex process, and certainly should be done with the proper support and strategies that are far beyond the purview of this book. Being aware that they exist, however, can be the first step on a Journey of its own.

> **Before You Move On:**
>
> Who are the Helpers and Mentors in your life? What have they contributed to your Journey? Be as specific as possible. Consider writing a thank you note letting them know that you appreciate their influence.

6. FACING THE MIRROR

I guess after Tommy was killed, Andy decided he'd been here just about long enough.

—"Red" Redding, *The Shawshank Redemption*
directed by Frank Darabont

Through the Trials and Temptations phase, the Hero of our story is gradually becoming better. They don't need as much help, they are more capable and knowledgeable, and life in general starts becoming easier. The confidence that comes with being able to function in the Unknown World is building, and things seem to be on an upward trajectory.

This upward swing can often feel like the Hero has passed through the most difficult parts of the Journey, and that life is going to get much easier from here. Unfortunately, Destiny has other plans for the Hero.

As much as the process of building skills and becoming more capable is an important part of the Journey, it is not the only part. True growth comes not just in adding skills and knowledge, it comes from eliminating the internal characteristics of the Hero that have become obsolete or counter-productive.

Much like a gardener who must prune back their trees for them to grow properly, the Hero is carrying with them qualities, ideas, and emotional burdens as part of their "inner self" that Destiny knows need to be removed for the Hero to truly progress. This is the purpose of the Abyss.

THE DEEP, DARK PIT

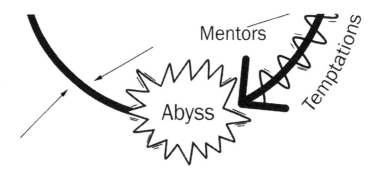

Much like the name suggests, the **Abyss** is connected with darkness, a sort of pit that the Hero must enter. Again, this can be a symbolic or a literal pit, but the emotion is the same regardless of the tangible experience.

The Abyss is the moment when the Hero hits rock bottom. They are at their most afraid, their most insecure, their most lonely—whatever negative quality has defined the Hero up to this point. It is in the Abyss that the Hero needs to face their true inner self, the one that they may have avoided acknowledging or dealing with since the beginning of the adventure.

In the Abyss, Destiny asks the Hero to make a sacrifice. Instead of giving up something tangible, the Hero is being asked to sacrifice a part of their inner self. These are traits, characteristics, mentalities, or behaviors that keep the Hero from achieving their true potential. They are often connected to deeper reasons the Hero felt unhappy at the beginning of the story.

To say that these sacrifices are difficult for the Hero would be an understatement. Whatever is being asked by Destiny as a sacrifice has served the Hero well in the past; letting go of that part of who they are is terrifying. Often their identity is intimately linked with this part of them. Giving it up means not only losing something comfortable and known but losing a part of who they perceive themselves to be. Destiny, always brutal in its honesty, is unapologetic for what it is asking the Hero to do.

SAD TO BE ALL ALONE IN THE WORLD

The decision to give up whatever Destiny is requiring is, ultimately, for the Hero to make. Mentors and Helpers cannot make the decision for the Hero, even if they happen to be present at the time. More often than not, you will find the Hero alone in these moments, stripped down of any exterior support. This seems to be a crucial aspect of Abyss moments, or at least symbolically appropriate for conveying the inner struggle of the Hero.

The temptation to choose either option—to sacrifice or not to sacrifice—must be equally strong on both sides. The reward for making the sacrifice must be equal to the price of making it. The larger the reward, the harder it will be for the Hero to give up those characteristics or behaviors. Were it not this way, the choice itself would offer a kind of support to, or manipulation of, the Hero. The pathways must be equally presented, and the Hero must choose which they will take.

EVERYONE'S INNOCENT IN HERE

An example of this can be seen in the character of Andy Dufresne from Stephen King's *The Shawshank Redemption*, referencing the film version where the filmmakers do a powerful job of showing us Andy's Abyss.

For Andy, going to Shawshank Prison is a terrible tragedy. Convicted of killing his wife and the man she was sleeping with, Andy insists from the beginning that he is innocent, only to be told that "everyone's innocent in here."

Gradually accepting his incarceration (though continuing his insistence that he is innocent), Andy becomes a force for good those working at the prison as well as in the lives of the inmates that become his close friends. He lobbies the state government for the books to start a library, helps inmates to pass a high school equivalency exam, and does tax preparation for the prison staff. Things begin to settle into a relatively positive experience.

The question of Andy's innocence comes to a head when a new inmate, Tommy, comes to Shawshank. Through a set of coincidences, not only does Tommy know that Andy is actually innocent, but he is willing and eager to testify to that fact. Hopeful that this could mean freedom, Andy goes to speak with the villain of the story, the corrupt Warden Samuel Norton.

Norton has been using Andy for years in money-making schemes and has no desire to lose his most profitable inmate. As Andy lays out his case, Warden Norton not only refuses to act on the information, he sends Andy to solitary for a month—longer than any punishment we have witnessed as an audience. In addition, with the discovery that Tommy's testimony might mean Andy's freedom, and that Norton's lucrative money laundering scheme would come to an end, Norton has Tommy killed in order to silence him permanently.

The Warden visits Andy in solitary to inform him that Tommy was killed trying to escape (something that Andy knows is false). Pale from the lack of sun and weak from a month of deprivation, you can see the toll that solitary has taken on him physically. You can also sense that mentally and emotionally it has been just as difficult for Andy. In anger, Andy tells Norton that he will no longer participate in the money laundering schemes.

Infuriated at Andy's defiance, Norton informs Andy that if he refuses to continue, not only will Andy lose his "protected" life and be thrown in with the hardened criminals, the warden will also destroy anything good that Andy had created. For extra good measure, Norton gives Andy another month in solitary to think it over.

This is Andy's Abyss. Two months in solitary in a literal dark hole, watching the possibility of freedom disappear, Andy hits rock bottom. He knows that any resistance to the warden's tyranny would result in not only harm to him but harm to his friends as well, and that adds to his despair.

This is a dark time for Andy, and the next time we see him after solitary, he is clearly changed, though it doesn't seem like a change for the better.

It is only later in the movie that we find out what choice Andy had to make in that Abyss: to stay at Shawshank or to go. In the Abyss, Andy is forced to decide whether to acquiesce to the warden's evil in exchange for the ability to continue to help his friends, or to finally act on his plan to escape from the prison.

In this case, it seems like Andy can no longer walk the thin line between good and evil. He now knows that the warden is pure evil, willing to kill in order to get what he wants, willing to hold the other inmates "hostage" to pursue his selfish scheme. Continuing to do as the warden demands would be submitting to evil. For Andy, a character who is good and hopeful and innocent of the crimes of which he is accused, submitting would mean the destruction of who he is.

Instead, he chooses to take his fate into his own hands and end the warden's reign of terror. This is the reward that the Abyss experience offers. The price that must be paid is the life, friends, and influence for good he has established during the previous decades.

Abyss experiences, as mentioned before, strip away the support systems and crutches that the Hero has relied upon up until this point. By taking everything away, by hitting rock bottom, the Hero is forced to stand on their own and choose: to make the sacrifice and move forward, or refuse the sacrifice and remain unchanged.

Without the time in the Abyss, it is unclear if Andy would have remained at Shawshank or not; with the Abyss, the decision that needs to be made is inevitable.

WATER, WATER EVERYWHERE

Let me pause the narrative for just a moment to add a very English-nerd point. As we know, for a Hero that is willing to make the sacrifice that is needed, the pathway leads out of the Abyss and on toward the end of the Journey. They enter the Journey as one thing and leave it as another. This movement from one state to another is often mirrored in the physical surroundings of the Abyss: water in some form or another.

For the Disney character Mulan, she experiences her Abyss while sitting on a snow-covered mountainside; Bilbo Baggins, main character of the Hobbit, experiences his Abyss at an underwater lake; even Harry Potter, living at a school of witchcraft and wizardry, experiences his Abyss looking into a mirror—a reflective surface similar to water.

This isn't too surprising since both water and the Abyss are symbolic of the same thing: death and rebirth. In the Abyss we see the death (either literal or symbolic) of the "old" Hero, and the birth of the "new" Hero. This new Hero has given up something that was holding them back and will forever be different than they were.

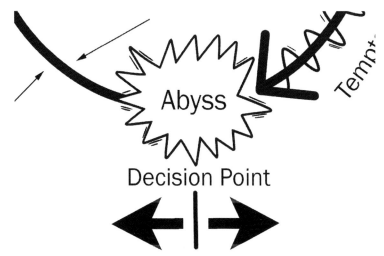

The Abyss is, ultimately, a Decision Point for the character. If they choose to make the sacrifice Destiny is asking, they will be able to move out of the Abyss and forward on their Journey. If they chose to reject the sacrifice, they will move backward on their Journey toward the beginning (this will be discussed more in depth in Chapter 11). The Abyss is a defining moment for the character, and the rest of their Journey is completely dependent upon what they do with the choice that is given to them.

Before You Move On:

Consider what Abyss moments you can identify. In what ways did the character(s) hit rock bottom? What choice were they asked to make? Was there any water symbolism (rain, snow, lakes, glass, etc.)?

REAL-WORLD JOURNEYS

Angela Duckworth, professor of psychology at the University of Pennsylvania and author of the best-selling book <u>Grit: The Power of Passion and Perseverance</u>, speaks about the neurobiology course she took in college. Confident in the beginning, it soon became clear that the class was beyond her, and her quiz and test scores showed it. After receiving advice from the teaching assistant that she should drop the course *and cut her losses, she thanked him and walked out of his office. Standing outside the door, Duckworth describes her experience this way:*

> *In the hallway, I surprised myself by not crying. Instead, I reviewed the facts of the situation: two failures, and only one more exam—the final—before the end of the semester. I realized I should have started out in a lower-level course, and now, more than halfway through the semester, it was obvious that my energetic studying wasn't proving sufficient. If I stayed, there was a good chance that I'd choke on the final and end up with an F on my transcript. If I dropped the course, I'd cut my losses.*
>
> *I curled my hands into fists, clenched my jaw, and marched directly to the registrar's office. At that moment, I'd resolved to stay enrolled in—and in fact, major in—neurobiology.*
>
> *Looking back on that pivotal day, I can see that I'd been knocked down—or, more accurately, tripped on my own two feet and fell flat on my face. Regardless, it was a moment when I could have stayed down. I could have said to myself: I'm an idiot! Nothing I do is good enough! And I could have dropped the class.*
>
> *Instead, my self-talk was defiantly hopeful: I won't quit! I can figure this out!*
>
> *For the rest of the semester, I not only tried harder, I tried things I hadn't done before. I went to every teaching assistants' office hours. I asked for extra work. I practiced doing the most difficult problems under time pressure—mimicking the conditions under which I needed to produce a flawless performance. I knew my nerves were going to be a problem at exam time, so I resolved to attain a level of mastery where nothing could surprise me. By the time the final exam came around, I felt like I could have written it myself.*
>
> *I aced the final. My overall grade in the course was a B-, the lowest grade I'd get in four years, but, ultimately, the one that made me proudest. (Grit, pp. 170-171)*

All of us can think of moments in our lives when we felt like we hit rock bottom. Whether emotionally, financially, occupationally, or more, these moments define us in ways that almost nothing else can.

Hitting rock bottom forces us to look honestly, sometimes for the first time, at the factors that led us to that point in our lives. The impetus for true, difficult change is powerful when the ugliness of our choices is staring us in the face. These are most definitely Abyss moments, and choosing the "other" path, sacrificing the part of ourselves that pulled us so far down, is as cathartic as it is difficult. We can almost feel the weight lifted off of our shoulders as we let go.

NOT ALWAYS DARK AND DREARY

While it is important to acknowledge dark and painful moments when they happen, you can have Abyss moments without having to hit rock bottom. Some Abyss moments simply ask us to look at negative qualities that we have and choose to act or react differently.

We all have these qualities. Perhaps we are impatient, insecure, afraid to commit, or selfish. Negative qualities can become very comfortable for us, even if they are not enjoyable. Our "natural" reaction to day-to-day circumstances is usually the result of years of choosing the path of least resistance; the longer we wait to change, the more difficult it is to break free of those patterns and habits. Whenever we are given the chance to choose a different action or reaction, and we choose it, we have successfully navigated an Abyss.

THE DARKNESS BEFORE THE LIGHT

There are also Abyss experiences where we are thrust into deep, dark places and stay for a long time. These can be intensely painful experiences as we wander in the darkness, unsure of what we are to do

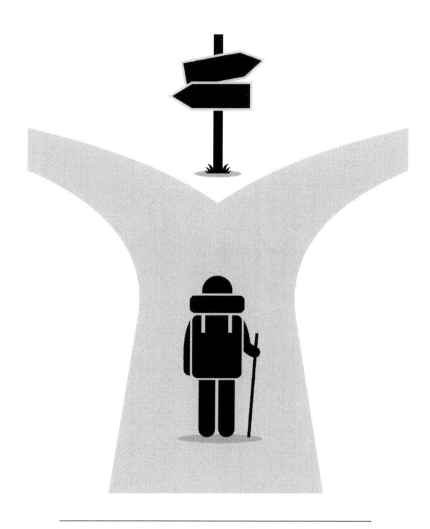

"One of the most difficult truths we have to accept about Abyss moments is that we do have a choice of some kind, and the choice holds the key to change."

or where we are to go. Sometimes these experiences are brought on through our own actions, sometimes the actions of others. Regardless of whether or not it is our fault we are in the Abyss, how we handle the experience is always within our power.

Sometimes in these moments, and often in the fallout afterward, we are left to determine how we are going to let our Abyss moments define us. The reality is that we still have choices in these moments. They are not choices that we necessarily want to make, but we have to make them. How we allow experiences define us can have a great impact on who we are and the Journeys that await us going forward.

One of the most difficult truths we have to accept about Abyss moments is that we do have a choice of some kind, and the choice holds the key to change. Often, we tell ourselves that we had no choice—that our agency was taken from us because we didn't choose this. This may be true about the events that led us to this moment, but within the Abyss itself, there is always a choice. As described by Angela Duckworth, standing outside the TA's office she was given a choice: to quit or to persevere. That choice defined her Journey. Our perspective may be limited, and our ability to discern those choices may be limited as well, but that does not mean those choices aren't there.

In reality, choice is one of the most important aspects of our existence. Viktor Frankl realized this truth during the horrors of life in a Nazi concentration camp. With everything taken away—home, family, culture, and even identity—Frankl found that he had one thing left: the ability to choose. He defined this as the ability-, "to choose one's attitude in any given set of circumstances, to choose one's own way" (*Man's Search for Meaning*, p. 86). When all else is gone, the ability to choose is still ours.

Perhaps we are not given the options we hoped for, or the options that we think we should have. If we learn to look closely there is always a choice presented in some form, even if it is just choosing our attitude toward our current situation.

THE IMPORTANCE OF ROCK BOTTOM

One final thought about this moment of hitting "rock bottom." Abyss moments are defining moments. The more difficult the choice to sacrifice, the more that choice defines us as we move forward on our own personal Hero's Journey.

Hitting rock bottom is sometimes the only way to get us to the point of making those sacrifices. As we hit this lowest point, we are usually left with nothing but ourselves and the truth. We are stripped of any exterior supports, including the lies we tell ourselves. There are times when we feel like we've hit rock bottom, only to find that there is more that we can lose.

This painful removal of the superficial and deceptive parts of ourselves leaves us raw, our perfect world now full of cracks. Once again, though, there is hope in this part of the process. Those cracks, as Leonard Cohen's song "Anthem" identifies, are "how the light gets in." The light from those cracks is illuminating something; we need to be courageous enough to look at what it is. Sometimes it takes hitting rock bottom to finally be able to see the way forward.

In a speech given in June of 2008 to a graduating class at Harvard, JK Rowling spoke of her own Abyss (not her word) and that experience of hitting rock bottom. She said that, for her,

> *...failure meant a stripping away of the inessential. I stopped pretending to myself that I was anything other than what I was, and began to direct all my energy into finishing the only work that mattered to me. Had I really succeeded at anything else, I might never have found the determination to succeed in the one arena I believed I truly belonged. I was set free, because my greatest fear had been realized, and I was still alive, and I still had a daughter whom I adored, and I had an old typewriter and a big idea. And so rock bottom became the solid foundation on which I rebuilt my life.*

In the midst of the darkness and humiliation and fear and despair, as we truly begin to let go, as we submit to the true power of the Journey process, we may just find ourselves standing, for the first time, on solid ground.

Before You Move On:

Abyss moments can vary in intensity, duration, and impact, and because of this they can be hard to identify. You might think of a time when you recognized something in yourself that needed to change, something that was difficult to give up. Or a time when you felt like you had hit rock bottom, and what that experience did for you. Take some time to write about an Abyss experience that you had, and what that experience did in defining your life today.

You might consider questions such as:

- What was your experience of the Abyss like emotionally?
- What was the choice that you were given?
- What was the sacrifice you had to make in order to move forward?

---

7. AT LAST I'VE SEEN THE LIGHT

If the fruit had a seed, it was the seed of my departure. The fruit was not a fruit. It was a dense accumulation of leaves glued together in a ball. The dozens of stems were dozens of leaf stems. Each stem that I pulled caused a leaf to peel off.

After a few layers, I came to leaves that had lost their stems and were flatly glued to the ball. I used my fingernails to catch their edges and pull them off. Sheath after sheath I lifted, like the skins off an onion...

...And then it came to light, an unspeakable pearl at the heart of a green oyster.

A human tooth.

—Pi Patel, *The Life of Pi* by Yann Martel

Surviving the Abyss experience is no easy feat, and Heroes often have "scars" to prove it. While there may not be physical scars, the effect on the Hero is very real, and the remnants of the sacrifice remain as a reminder of the ordeal.

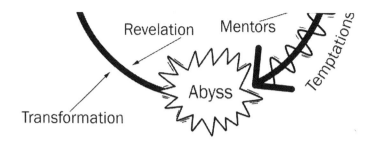

Connected with the Abyss are two notable events that are essential in the progress of the Hero: the **Revelation** and the **Transformation**. In some stories they actually happen in the Abyss, but they may happen at a different time, so we will discuss them separately.

REVELATION

As the Hero makes progress on their Journey, one of the defining moments for the Hero is when they receive what we call a Revelation. The Hero must, at some point, start seeing the world differently than they did before, and the Journey process facilitates this change in perspective.

The Revelation may mean learning a truth that was hidden before, gaining clarity regarding something they had been confused about, or maybe a change in perspective that opens up a whole new understanding of the path they are on. This revelatory information is life-altering. The world makes more sense now, the path seems clearer, the destination is finally in sight.

A SHADOW OF PARADISE

For Pi Patel, the main character in *The Life of Pi*, his life is turned upside down when the ship his family is sailing on sinks and the only survivors on the lifeboat are Pi and a tiger named Richard Parker. Pi's process of surviving and his adventures with Richard Parker ultimately lead them to an island in the middle of the ocean. At first, Pi stays close to the boat and sleeps in the trees, with Richard Parker sleeping in the boat. Gradually, as food is plentiful, Pi restores his strength and is able to explore further and further into the island.

The further he goes the more Pi begins to realize that this island is almost perfect. There is enough food for him and Richard Parker, clean water, and no visible predators. He begins to imagine that this could be a place that he could stay and live for a long time.

Unfortunately for Pi, the island has a sinister secret that he discovers. After picking a berry and peeling back the skin, Pi sees that enveloped within the berry is a human tooth. At that moment, Pi realizes that the island is not what it seems. Far from being a paradise, the island is a predator in and of itself. Each night the ground becomes lethal, consuming anything on, or below, the surface.

This Revelation shatters Pi's dreams of finding a place to settle that falls short of his ultimate goal of returning home. What seemed like a paradise is revealed to be a death trap, and that knowledge cannot be un-seen. If Pi stays, he will die.

Armed with that knowledge, he also determines that he can't leave Richard Parker on the island. Without the boat to sleep in, the tiger will also be consumed. The knowledge revealed on the island not only saves Pi's life, but also marks a turning point for the relationship between him and the tiger.

ECHOES OF WISDOM

As much as there is no Mentor present for Pi, the influence of Mentors plays a large role in many literary Revelations. At times, the Mentor knows that the Hero is facing an Abyss moment and offer words of perspective that change the way the Hero sees the world.

In other stories, it is the words of a Mentor that come back to the Hero at a crucial moment. If those words don't change the Hero when they are first spoken, the Hero will be reminded of them at the exact moment when they need them most. This could be a song that used to be sung, a verse that was repeated over and over, a motto that was hung up on the wall. In a moment the words become infinitely more meaningful than they could have been before the Hero embarked on their Journey.

TRANSFORMATION

The combined experience of the Abyss and the Revelation lead to a Transformation: the Hero becomes different than they were before. They will, by the nature of their Trials and their experience in the Abyss, change into something more than they could have been otherwise.

The Transformation is the culmination of all the experiences the Hero has gone through on their Journey, specifically the sacrifice that was made in the Abyss. We, as the audience, can see the difference. They are more courageous, or more confident, or more knowledgeable, or more (fill-in-the-blank for whatever character trait) than they were before.

Often it is not just the audience that notices—other characters in the story may be able to see the change as well. Regardless, Heroes that enter the Abyss and come out the other side do so having left the old Hero behind. The world of the Hero, and the Hero themselves, are permanently Transformed.

YOU SEEM DIFFERENT SOMEHOW

For Pi, the changes are internal but important. His acceptance of Richard Parker, of the relationship that has kept them both alive, and of his determination to get them both home is all sealed. The way he talks, the way we get to see his view of the situation, has changed, and the Transformation is crucial for Pi's, and Richard Parker's, survival.

A few characters undergo an actual physical transformation. Gandalf, of the *Lord of the Rings* trilogy, is an interesting example of this. Acting as a Mentor for Frodo up until the point he disappears into the Abyss with a menacing creature known as the Balrog, Gandalf embarks upon a Journey of his own—one that begins with his own literal death. As Gandalf the Grey dies, Gandalf the White is born. He is different than the previous iteration, and the Transformation is both external (the change in "color") as well as internal (he is more powerful).

FLUID RELATIONSHIPS

As you examine stories that you are familiar with, you may find that the actual placement of the Abyss, the Revelation, and the Transformation may vary. The Abyss might actually come quite early, and the Revelation/Transformation quite late. Or perhaps the Trials and Temptations last for most of the story, with the Abyss, Revelation, and Transformation happening quickly right before the end. There are some stories where the Revelation brings about the Abyss, with the Transformation close behind. The specific placement of these events is not what matters; what matters are the experiences that prepare the Hero for what is to come.

Before You Move On:

Think about the changes and Transformations that came upon characters you are familiar with. What change in perspective did they receive? How did their experience in the Abyss, coupled with their Revelation, Transform them? Did other characters notice the change?

REAL-WORLD JOURNEYS

The story of Helen Keller is well-known, and her relationship with her teacher is often used as an example of a powerful Mentor relationship. Struck deaf and blind at the age of one, the first years of Helen's life were filled with confusion and darkness. When Helen's parents hired a teacher for her, they were looking for someone to reach her.

Anne Sullivan was Helen's Teacher/Mentor, who had tried a few different teaching tactics, but Helen seemed only able to mimic the movements Anne was trying to teach. She did not understand what was being communicated. One day, Anne had an idea. Coming to the room where Helen was playing, Anne took her by the hand.

"We walked down the path to the well-house... attracted by the fragrance of the honeysuckle with which it was covered. Someone was drawing water and my teacher placed my hand under the spout. As the cool stream gushed over one hand she spelled into the other the word water, first slowly, then rapidly. I stood still, my whole attention fixed upon the motions of her fingers. Suddenly I felt a misty consciousness as of something forgotten—a thrill of returning thought; and somehow the mystery of language was revealed to me. I knew then that "w-a-t-e-r" meant the wonderful cool something that was flowing over my hand. That living word awakened my soul, gave it light, hope, joy, set it free! There were barriers still, it is true, but barriers that could in time be swept away."

—Helen Keller, *The Story of My Life*

The experience of the Abyss is transformative enough, though what you walk away with can feel more like battle wounds than anything else. With a successful Abyss experience you are primed and ready to be able to reap the rewards of your hard, and often painful, work.

Our Journeys present us with a great many opportunities to learn and grow. The process of working through the Trials and Temptations expands our understanding and our knowledge, we learn new skills, and we become better and more capable. However, what we learn in the Trials step is not the same as what we learn through our Abyss experience. Just as in literature, part of the learning and growth of the Abyss is tied to our own Revelations and Transformations.

PREPARED TO SEE

A Revelation comes in a moment when we are finally able to see whatever it is we need to see. The changes that we have experienced and the sacrifices we have made, help us to make connections and comprehend ideas that we were not able to do before. We may even come up with new ideas that answer questions we have had or problems we've been trying to solve.

The key with Revelations is that the person we were before all of these experiences occurred could not understand the knowledge being presented. Parents often have experiences where a child excitedly tells them something they "just learned," when in reality the parents have been telling their child that exact same thing for years. The work the parent did was crucial in helping to build the child's ability to understand, but until the child is ready, the understanding itself cannot take place.

When we are prepared, Revelations can come into our lives. They are empowering and can be the key to enabling us to complete the unique task that is waiting.

IN ITS OWN SWEET TIME, THANK YOU VERY MUCH

The Revelations we receive often come at unexpected times. As comedian, writer, and producer Tina Fey was learning to balance taking care of her young daughter's needs with her own apprehension at asking the nanny to do things differently, she noted the strange timing of these experiences. She observes,

> *"This is one of the weirdest things about motherhood. You can't predict that some of your best moments will happen around the toilet at six a.m. while you're holding a pile of fingernail clippings like a Santeria priestess."*

> (*Bossypants, p. 260*)

Many people talk about ideas coming to them in the shower, or when they are taking a walk, or going for a drive. Having experienced this myself, I can attest to its truthfulness.

We cannot forget that the Revelation can only come AFTER we have put in the work. We can't figure out the solution to a problem we

"She no longer saw herself as destined to fail.
She had power over the outcome of her story."

haven't pondered. We can't come up with a new way to do things without thoroughly studying the way things are already done. Don't fall into the trap of thinking that people who have great ideas are just sitting around waiting for something to fall into their lap. Revelations of this type are the end result of a great deal of pondering, questioning, trial and error, and researching.

The preliminary work that happens during the Trials and Temptations phase is preparing us to understand larger and deeper truths that we were unable to comprehend before. When the clouds finally part and the sun shines through, it is a powerful experience.

The student that I mentioned in the Introduction to this book experienced a Revelation there in class. As she examined her experience through this new lens, she was able to see her actions in a new light. She no longer saw herself as destined to fail. She had power over the outcome of her story. Recognizing why things had not gone the way she had hoped, she felt confident that her new understanding would allow her story to turn out differently this time.

THE MAN IN THE MOON

Revelations change the way we see the world, and the change is permanent. Even if, for some reason, we determine not to ultimately embrace the changes that were a part of the Abyss, that new understanding or perspective stays with us.

I remember being eleven years old when I first saw the "Man in the Moon." I had heard people talk about it, and I decided one night to try and find what people were talking about. Looking at the moon was something I had always enjoyed. Seeing the craters, the shadows, all of it was fascinating to me.

When I finally was able to see the face, it was exciting. Now, decades later, each time I look at the moon, that is what I see. For better or for worse, I can't "unsee" it.

We will have Revelations in our lives that we will wish we could "unsee." Sometimes knowing something means we have an obligation to act when taking action would be difficult. Sometimes knowing something means we should treat others differently because now we understand them better. And, sometimes knowing something means the loss of innocence, leaving us with a longing to go back to the way things were.

In spite of this, the Revelation is an important building block for future growth. Whether it sets us free or slaps us in the face, our new understanding is crucial to moving forward.

TRANSFORMATION

Transformation comes as we move to fill the new shape of our understanding and experience. Our capacity has been expanded because of what we have seen and done, and we have likely had to give up character flaws and limiting beliefs that held us back. The desire to act on these changes feels like freedom, and we know that we are different than we were before.

For Helen Keller, the moment she understood that what her teacher was doing was more than just random movement with her fingers, the whole world opened up to her. That knowledge allowed her to break free of the symbolic darkness of her disability and become thirsty to learn anything and everything she could.

A similar experience is recounted by Daniel James Brown in *Boys in the Boat,* the story of the 1936 Olympic rowing team. Brown focuses the book on the story of Joe Rantz, a poor boy with a difficult childhood who found solace and belonging on the rowing team at the University of Washington. As Joe and his team were preparing to compete in a series of races that could land them in the 1936 Olympics, he was struggling to find his place. He had been rejected as a child by his stepmother and, to a lesser degree, his father. He had trust issues, not wanting to be hurt as he had been so many times before.

George Pocock, a Mentor and friend to this team from the University of Washington, spoke to Joe after observing his rowing for some time. Pocock knew that Joe was extremely talented, and that this team had something special if it could pull together. Brown recounts the conversation between the two of them as Pocock told Joe,

> *"there were times when (Joe) seemed to think he was the only fellow in the boat, as if it was up to him to row the boat across the finish line all by himself. When a man rowed like that, he said, he was bound to attack the water rather than work with it, and worse, he was bound not to let his crew help him row."*

Pocock then suggested that Joe:

> *"think of a well-rowed race as a symphony, and himself as just one player in the orchestra. If one fellow in an orchestra was playing out of tune, or playing at a different tempo, the whole piece would naturally be ruined. That's the way it was with rowing. What mattered more than how hard a man rowed was how well everything he did in the boat harmonized with what the other fellows were doing. And a man couldn't harmonize with his crewmates unless he opened his heart to them. He had to care about his crew. It wasn't just the rowing but his crewmates that he had to give himself up to, even if it meant getting his feelings hurt."*

> *(Boys in the Boat, pp. 234-235)*

That understanding changed Joe, and it changed his rowing. From that day, he found his stroke, settled in with the rest of the boys in the boat, and they worked as a team to beat the odds and take the gold medal in the Berlin Olympics.

A WHOLE NEW WORLD

Revelations open the door for change to occur. Not just any change, but substantive, necessary change. These may be changes that we have needed to make for a long time, but something was blocking the change from truly taking hold.

Transformation comes when we have let go of the very things that have been holding us back, things that may have been comfortable and familiar, but were preventing our growth. Journeys bring these experiences and opportunities to the forefront, but we have to act on them.

This cumulative process that starts with the Abyss and moves through the Revelation and the Transformation, results in a completely different person coming out on the other side. That person is exactly who the Journey is preparing us to be.

Before You Move On:

Take some time to reflect on the ways you were changed through Journeys of your own. Can you track the difference between the you that started the Journey and the one who finished? Take some time to write about some of these experiences.

Consider the following questions:

- What did you learn through the experience?
- How did your vision or understanding of the Journey, yourself, others, and/or the world change through this experience?
- How did the experience change you?

---

8. GAME. SET. MATCH.

Sometimes the world seems against you
The Journey may leave a scar
But scars can heal and reveal
Just where you are
The people you love will change you
The things you have learned will guide you
And nothing on earth can silence
The quiet voice still inside you
And when that voice starts to whisper
Moana, you've come so far
Moana, listen
Do you know who you are?

—Gramma Tala, *Moana* directed by Ron Clements

Once the Hero has completed their Transformation, they are finally ready to take on the event that the Journey has been preparing them for: the *Unique Task*. In fact, the Journey has been preparing the Hero in very specific ways, so specific that ultimately the Hero is the only one who can accomplish this task. It is unique to them, and they must be the one to complete it.

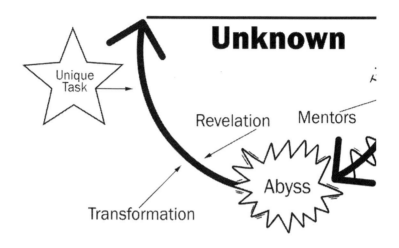

This moment in the story tends to be the most exciting, the most intense. In other circumstances we would call this part the climax of the story: the moment when all the forces come together to determine the final outcome.

At this point, the outcome is still uncertain. The coming army is enormous. The villain is frighteningly powerful. The opposing team has been called "unbeatable." What the Hero is facing is not simple or easy. The key, however, is that the Hero has been prepared to face the task in their own, unique way. It is their experience, their personality, their power that is needed in this moment, and no one else's. The Hero brings something to the table that no one else can offer, and that something is the key to victory.

Of course, that doesn't mean it will be a walk in the park, and that there won't be loss or damage on the way to the conclusion. It doesn't even mean that the Hero feels ready, or that they will even "succeed" at the Task that is given, though the definition of "success" is different depending on who is defining it.

What it does mean is that the Journey has been geared toward preparing for a singular event, and if the Hero has learned and sacrificed and transformed appropriately, they are absolutely capable of accomplishing what is necessary.

THE GIRL FROM THE ISLAND

Moana set out from her island with a very specific mission: find the demi-god Maui and take him across the ocean so he can defeat the monster Te Ka and restore the "Heart of Te Fiti" (which he'd stolen centuries before). Through the process of finding and traveling with Maui, Moana learns and grows a great deal, becomes much more capable, and, after a powerful Abyss/Revelation/Transformation experience with her grandmother, sheds her insecurity and commits to her destiny. Moana, not Maui, is the one who needs to restore the heart.

Armed with this confidence, Moana returns to accomplish this Unique Task, using everything she has learned to take on Te Ka. With Maui there to help, they get Moana past the barrier and she runs to restore the heart. Upon reaching the crest of the hill, though, she looks down to see that Te Fiti is not where they thought she would be. Moana realizes that the creature they were battling was actually Te Fiti, turned monstrous after her heart was stolen.

Going into this final battle, all the assumptions were that Te Ka was the obstacle to reaching Te Fiti. However, because of what Moana had gone through, particularly her own Journey to discover that power comes from knowing who you truly are, she is able to recognize the truth of who Te Ka is. She is then able to get Te Ka/Te Fiti to see that the rage and the anger are not what define her, and to help her remember who she really is.

The power of this moment is what speaks to the uniqueness of this Task for Moana. The understanding that she gained on the Journey was exactly what was needed to help restore the heart. Maui could not have done it; his solution would be to trick and to fight his way to victory. Neither of those strategies would have worked.

Moana was uniquely prepared, and because of a combination of both her life on the island and her adventure on the sea, she and she alone is able to restore the Heart and save the islands.

FULFILLING A PROMISE

Now, this is the moment where we need to revisit some of the things that I said we would come back to way back at the beginning of the book. As we discussed the beginning of the Journey Model, we talked about how we are able to observe the Hero at their starting point. We get to see the world they are living in, the people they associate with, and the choices they make in their lives. We referred to that as "establishing a baseline." The Unique Task is where I promised that we'd see where the baseline matters.

As we compare the Hero that left home with the Hero that is now facing this daunting task, we can see the amount of change and improvement that has happened through the course of the Journey. Often the Hero that we started with and the Hero we have before us now are so different, it is hard to believe that they are the same person. That is why the baseline matters—it allows us to see the ways in which the Hero has changed, and the meaning behind those changes.

The second thing I want to go back to is the purpose of the Journey. I mentioned briefly that there are times when the Hero thought they knew what the end of the Journey would be but are often mistaken. A character leaves home thinking he is going to start a business to make millions, only to discover that what he really needed was to change his priorities. An athlete thinks she is destined to win the championship, but instead finds out that she would rather do something else with her life.

Again, this isn't always the case, but often the Hero has such a narrow view of what they are capable of accomplishing (or even what is out there in the world), that the Unique Task isn't even on their radar. Moana was sure that Maui was the one who needed to restore the heart. It never occurred to her that she could be capable of accomplishing such a feat.

There are Journeys where Destiny has something much larger, much more important in mind than the Hero can anticipate, adding an extra level of excitement and fulfillment when the Task is revealed and the Hero is left to see how they are equal to the task.

There are also Journeys where the Hero doesn't understand the Unique Task until much later. Perspective is a powerful tool, but the cost is often patience and experience. Perhaps they lost the national championship, only to realize later that learning how to lose was a crucial lesson in their growth. These experiences may have one meaning in the moment, and then a different or refined meaning later.

It does seem a bit anticlimactic that, at what seems to be the most exciting and tense part of the story, there doesn't seem to be much to say about it. Unique Tasks can be exciting, intense, emotional, and more. The point is that the Hero has everything they need to accomplish the Task. So, sit back and enjoy the ride.

Before You Move On:

Take this chance to do a comparison of a character who started a Journey, and the character that takes on their Unique Task. What are the differences between the two? How did the Journey prepare the character? What was the Unique Task, and did the Hero know what it was going to be?

REAL-WORLD JOURNEYS

The start of Dwight D. Eisenhower's military career was rather lackluster, and he bounced around without any real direction or ambition. He joined the conflict in Europe right at the end of World War I, was denied an assignment in Europe, and was unable make any substantive contribution.

A few years passed, and he continued to make only marginal progress toward any sort of leadership position. In 1928, he was given an assignment that, on the surface, would seem trivial. Eisenhower was helped by a mentor to get assigned to the American Battle Monuments Commission where he served until 1929. The American Battle Monuments Commission "administers, operates, and maintains permanent U.S. military cemeteries, memorials and monuments both inside and outside the United States." This wasn't exactly an obvious path toward leadership.

During the first six months of his time with the Commission, he studied the battles of World War I and knew them well enough to produce <u>A Guide to the American Battle Fields in Europe,</u> which demonstrated an understanding of General Pershing's strategies that was second only to Pershing himself. He spent time walking the battlefields in France, studying WWI's most important landscapes, roads, and strategic locations as part of this assignment.

In 1930, as the U.S. government determined that another war could indeed be on the horizon, they began to make plans for mobilization should such an event occur. Eisenhower was assigned to accompany General George Van Horn Moseley to travel across the country to evaluate the industrial capacity of various sites. Because of this trip, he expanded his understanding of what the U.S. manufacturing sector could accomplish.

From 1936-38, Eisenhower worked closely with General Douglas McArthur as an aide, a time that Eisenhower did not look back on fondly. Referring to the two years as "slavery," he watched the general and determined very quickly that he did not agree with McArthur's style of command, though this opportunity did give him a chance to learn how to work with difficult personalities. He developed his own style in response to this experience that was almost opposite of what he had observed.

Taken as individual experiences, it would seem that Eisenhower did not have much going for him, let alone the potential to be in command of the army during one of the most dangerous and crucial wars in world history. However, seen as a whole, it becomes clear that Eisenhower was prepared in such a unique and powerful way, that there was literally no one else who could do what he did.

Eisenhower was the only one with the perspective of the strategies, players, and physical landscape of Europe. He had the understanding of what the country would be capable of producing to support the war effort. He had the command style that led an army to trust and follow him, and deal with strong personalities like Churchill, Patton, Marshall, and Montgomery.

According to one Air Force colonel, "It wasn't like he was one of a thousand or even a hundred who were capable of doing what he did. He was literally one of one. No one else could have done what he did the way he did it."

The circumstances that we find ourselves facing when we hit the Unique Task are often so urgent or important that we don't always get a chance in the moment to reflect on the steps that led us there. The Tasks that are a part of our Journey are intended specifically for us, and the unique mixture of personality, experience, knowledge, temperament, and more make us the "chosen one" for our particular Journey. We see this with Eisenhower. With time and hindsight, we can often identify the major experiences—both successes and failures—that have led us to where we are.

When it comes to finally accomplishing the purpose of our Journey, the experience can range from world-changing to barely creating a ripple. Some of us are destined to take on enemies that threaten thousands of others; some of us are tasked with facing our personal demons. The magnitude is unimportant. What matters is that we can look back and clearly see the steps that have led us to this moment, and we know that we are capable. The moment is here, it is ours for the taking, and the prices paid show themselves to be worth the pain.

Eisenhower is a somewhat extreme example, seeing as how his Unique Task was to lead the military forces of a world power during a major war. Most of us will not have that sort of burden.

The Journey that Maya Angelou undertakes in her book *The Heart of a Woman* seems, in many ways, to be her process of self-discovery and empowerment as a woman and as a person of African descent. Clearly the larger message of the book, there is plenty to learn from this.

But there is also an interesting, subtle Journey that she embarks upon—one that does not reach its culmination until the very last paragraphs of the book. As Maya has traveled through heartache, from California to New York to Egypt, from one man to another, from one disappointment to another, the one constant through the process has been her son Gus. Always somewhere on the periphery, Gus' security, his happiness, his struggles, are somewhere in the considerations that Maya tries to reconcile.

As we reach the end of the book, with Maya facing a new life yet again, the last few words are dedicated to the moment when her son, this constant presence, leaves to go off to college. She hugs him goodbye, watches him drive away, and then steps back inside.

In that moment she remembers:

> *I closed the door and held my breath. Waiting for the wave of emotion to surge over me, knock me down, take my breath away. Nothing happened. I didn't feel bereft or desolate. I didn't feel lonely or abandoned.*

> *I sat down, still waiting. The first thought that came to me, perfectly formed and promising, was "At last, I'll be able to eat the whole breast of a roast chicken by myself."*

> *(The Heart of a Woman, p.336)*

If it is possible, all the pain and the struggle and the uncertainty that Maya conquered in so many facets of her life made her strong enough to not just overcome the great obstacles that came into her life, but also to be able to say goodbye to her son. The constant, the one that she relied upon in many ways as she struggled to be a good mother, was leaving her, and it had the potential to overcome her. And yet, it didn't. She was ready.

Maya did not know she was ready until that very moment, and that understanding came almost as a surprise. But she faced the moment, she stared that dragon in the face, and was able to stand in her power and not be overwhelmed by the experience.

I don't know that Maya would see the same things in this experience, but her words convey the power of that moment for her. This applies to each of us. The scale of the Task is unimportant; the process for becoming prepared for what lies ahead of us is what matters.

Our Unique Tasks are aligned with the Journey we have experienced, the Trials we have faced, the successes and failures, and the things we are willing to give up in order to progress. As we trust the process and learn and grow with each experience, we will be prepared when it is our turn to step into the spotlight.

WHY WE PLAY THE GAME

Arriving at the moment that this Journey has been building towards is fulfilling and thrilling. All the hard work, all the sacrifices, all the heartache, finally have a purpose. We reach the moment that we have been waiting for, and the climax of all the experiences we have gone through.

You would think, after going through the entire process, that we could just put a check in the "Win" column and move on with our lives. We must be careful, though. As much as we are prepared for the Task ahead because of everything we have gone through, that doesn't mean

"All the hard work, all the sacrifices, all the heartache, finally have a purpose."

we can predict the outcome with certainty.

I remember a conversation I had with one of my students after talking about these concepts in class. She had been a tennis player since she was young and was ready to dismiss the Journey process altogether because, as she put it, "If you are right, I should win every match I play." For her, all the work, all the preparation, all the sacrifice, could only have one acceptable outcome: winning the match. Winning *every* match.

This is an easy trap to fall into, and one that we have to be very wary of. In the grand scheme of things, "winning" is not necessarily a black and white concept where either you win or you don't. While in competitive sports there is a clear winner to the match (most of the time), winning may look very different to different people. Beating a personal record can be just as fulfilling (if not more so) than coming in first. Finishing the race may be just as momentous as a gold medal.

Much of how the Task is viewed depends on the attitude of the competitor. As Pierre de Coubertin (father of the modern Olympics) said, "The important thing in the Olympic Games is not to win, but to take part; the important thing in Life is not triumph, but the struggle; the essential thing is not to have conquered but to have fought well."

While there may be those that would look at that quote and declare, "That kind of thinking is for losers," this may be missing the point. The point of the Journey is not to win, the point is to become capable of winning. Or to become capable of surviving if you don't win. Or to build friendships through the process that can last a lifetime—completely separate from winning at all.

There are so many potential ways to have a successful Journey; it is important not to put superficial boundaries around our definition of success that can obscure what we have actually accomplished. If we define success with a number, a date, a size, etc., we ignore the actual success we can experience every day—success in the form of progress.

YOU CAN'T SKIP TO THE END

The Unique Task only matters if you have gone through the entire process of the Journey. Skipping to the end, finding success without paying the price, leads to questionable victories. Victories that are won without struggle are unsustainable at best. When faced with tougher, or even similar, tests, the outcome can just as easily be failure. Only those who have truly gone through the process to become capable of being victorious, who have paid the price to progress to that level, can compete with any consistency.

We see many situations in our society where we mistake the point of the Journey as being the Unique Task instead of the growth and improvement necessary to complete that Task. In doing so, we sabotage our own progress. For individuals trying to skip the work of the Trials to get to the Task, this is where lying, cheating, stealing, and other similar behaviors come to bear.

Unwilling, or afraid, to face the reality of how progress and change actually work, we sometimes try to skip to the end of the process, thinking that somehow it will be better. It may actually be better in the short-term. In the long-term, though, these behaviors are not only unsustainable, but actually deny us real, meaningful progress.

This problem does not just plague individuals on their Journeys, though. Mentors often make the mistake of trying to get the Hero to the Unique Task as quickly, or as painlessly, as possible. Some parents, hoping to help their children to avoid failure, remove any obstacles that may be placed in their children's way. In their minds, the point of the Journey is to get into college, or to get a certain job.

Unfortunately, they forget that the actual point is to become capable of handling college or succeeding at any job. College or jobs are vehicles, not destinations. If a child gets into college but has no skill set, no knowledge base, and no understanding of societies or systems, they will fail. Getting into college is not the point; being able to succeed in college is the point.

It's not just parents that do this. Teachers do it, coaches do it, employers do it. This is particularly true in any situation where the Mentor is feeling pressure to create a specific outcome. They lose sight of the point of the Journey and their role within it, and the results are often heartbreaking.

LOOKING PAST THE UNIQUE TASK

With the right mindset, the Unique Task can be fulfilling regardless of the outcome. To become capable of succeeding means developing a certain set of skills or knowledge base. The skills and knowledge often transcend any particular moment or Task and are useful well beyond a singular event.

You see, we get to take the skills and knowledge with us as we move forward. If we have struggled and transformed, they are now a part of us. Chances are good that they will be useful to us many times over as we continue to grow and progress, not just as tools for certain circumstances, but as foundations for future knowledge and skills. That is the beauty of the process: it prepares us not just for right now, but also for things well beyond our current ability to comprehend.

Before You Move On:

Take some time to consider what Unique Tasks you might have experienced, as well as the Journey that led you to being able to face those Tasks. Write down your thoughts and feelings about the process and how you changed. Consider the following:

- What was the Task that the Journey was leading toward?
- Was it what you thought it would be when you set out?
- How did the Journey prepare you for the Task?
- What was the end result?

---

9. YOU CAN'T STEP IN THE SAME RIVER

"Are you in pain, Frodo?" said Gandalf quietly as he rode by Frodo's side.

"Well, yes I am," said Frodo. "It is my shoulder. The wound aches, and the memory of darkness is heavy on me. It was a year ago today."

"Alas! There are some wounds that cannot be wholly cured," said Gandalf.

"I fear it may be so with mine," said Frodo. "There is no real going back. Though I may come to the Shire, it will not seem the same; for I shall not be the same."

—*The Return of the King* by JRR Tolkien

With the Unique Task finally completed, the purpose of their Journey finally fulfilled, it seems important for us to ask: what comes next? Generally speaking, after the climax of the story, the intensity and urgency abates. Wrongs have been righted, enemies conquered, loves found, so what comes next is the task of living with the consequences.

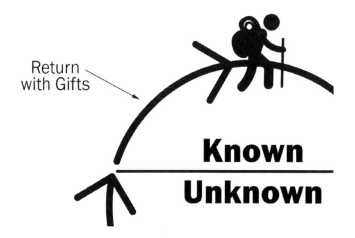

This phase in the Journey sees the Hero going home, back to those that knew them before. After completing their unique task, they cross back over the Threshold, this time going from the Unknown World (which is now much more "known"), back to the Known World from before. This crossing is called *The Return*, and the Hero does so bringing with them the gifts and rewards of their Journey.

THE GIFTS OF THE JOURNEY

The hero may have received tangible gifts (a sword, a book of spells, a ring on their finger, etc.). Yet, the most important gifts that the Journey gives are internal. The Hero comes home more confident, wiser, more patient, kinder, etc. These gifts come as a natural extension of the Hero's actions and experiences. The gifts feel warranted, earned, and deserved.

More than just the Gifts that the Hero enjoys, there are Gifts for those at home as well. You see, incumbent upon the Hero receiving these Gifts is the understanding that they now have a duty to use those very Gifts to help those that are around them. This is a sacred obligation, and to understand that the Gifts are meant for lifting and helping those around is to glimpse the far-reaching perspective of the Journeys we take. We are, quite literally, being prepared to help those that are around us. Gifts are never to be concealed or used selfishly; they are always for a larger purpose.

THE THREE TYPES OF RETURNS

While it seems like going home should be rather straight-forward, it can be a complex situation. Since the Hero, literally, cannot step into the same river twice, returning home means facing change yet again.

The Return occurs most often in one of three ways. Which of the three the Hero experiences is determined by two factors. First, the commitment of the Hero to maintaining the changes they have experienced. Second, the amount of friction caused by the difference between who the Hero has become and the state of those they come home to.

For the purposes of this discussion, we will assume that the Hero is committed to maintaining the changes that have occurred. A discussion about those who surrender those changes can be found in Chapter 11. Assuming, however, that they will fight to maintain those changes, let's look at how the second factor—friction—impacts the Hero's experience of Returning home.

VERSION #1: HAPPILY EVER AFTER

The "happily ever after" version sees the Hero coming home to a hero's welcome, joy, adulation, ticker-tape parades, and similar events. The person that the Hero has become is honored and respected, and the changes are most welcome. Everyone is happy with this new, transformed Hero, and the Heroes themselves are prepared to step into a role that seems to be waiting for them.

With this type of Return, there is almost no friction between the Hero and the people they return to. Their ability to remain their new, transformed self meets with almost no resistance, and the changes that they have made are supported and sustained. You often see these types of Returns in coming-of-age stories, where the Hero needs to enter the adult world, and is welcomed when they do so. This is the type of coming home that we would imagine and hope for our Hero.

VERSION #2: SQUARE PEG, ROUND HOLE

The "Square Peg, Round Hole" version is the exact opposite of the previous version. As opposed to a warm welcome and "happily ever after," the Hero is so changed and so different that they do not fit back into the society that they left. There is no new role for them to step into, no place for the transformed Hero to belong.

In addition, there is intense friction between the person they have become and the world they are returning to, with powerful pressure from those at home for the Hero to go back to the way they were before the Journey. Perhaps the new Hero threatens to expose truths at home that others don't want to hear. Maybe the changes the Hero has made run in contrast to the home culture. And, quite possibly, the Hero now sees the world in such a way that they can't "unsee," but those at home are not ready for the new perspective.

Ultimately, the end result of this type of Return is that the Hero, in order to maintain the changes they have made in themselves, must leave home again. The friction is too intense, the pressure too great, for the Hero to be able to stay and also be happy and fulfilled. When this happens, leaving is the best option. The Hero will need to seek out another "home" that will support and nurture them so that they can continue to progress.

VERSION #3: THE BRIDGE

The third version is a combination of the two previous versions. The Hero is not rejected by those at home, but at the same time, the changes that have been made are more than they at home can understand. The Hero will often experience friction and pressure in many ways to go back to being who they were before because people automatically expect them to step back in to whatever role they previously occupied.

Again, the Hero needs to decide if they want to maintain the changes or succumb to the pressure to revert in order to get rid of the friction. In this case, specifically because of the changes that were made in the Hero, they are ultimately able to create a "Bridge" between themselves and the world they are returning to.

Using the knowledge and skills the Hero gained on the Journey, they can create a new role for themselves—the Bridge—to find a place where they can now belong. They carve out a place for themselves that can be honored and respected by the society, and the role is also fulfilling for the Hero.

THREE RETURNS IN ONE

For simplicity's sake, the example that I use for this step in the Journey actually contains all three versions of the Return experience. The film version of *The Return of the King* is an epic story that pulls off this rare feat. In this case, we will focus on the Hobbits and their experience of the Return. A different discussion could be had about the endings in the book, but the movie supplies what we need in a clear, straightforward way.

Once Sauron has been defeated and the world has been saved from darkness, the main characters in the movie come together in Minas Tirith to start the healing process and to move forward with life after this great adventure. After Aragorn has taken his rightful place as High King of Gondor and we have a resolution of his relationship with Arwen, the two of them walk through the crowd to where the Hobbits are standing. The four Hobbits see him coming and begin to bow to Aragorn, but he stops them.

"My friends," he says quickly, "you bow to no one." The king himself then bows out of respect for what these four seemingly insignificant Hobbits have done to save the world. The rest of the crowd follows suit.

The respect that the Hobbits are shown by those at Minas Tirith is an example of the Happily Ever After version of the Return. Not only do the people of Minas Tirith know what the Hobbits have gone through and sacrificed, they respect the Hobbits for it. There is no friction here—Frodo, Sam, Merry, and Pippin are honored exactly for who they are (or who they have become on the Journey) and no one there resents those changes or wishes that they would go back to who they were before.

Upon returning to the Shire, however, things are not exactly as smooth. We see this in a scene that takes place shortly after they return. As they sit together at the pub, surrounded by others who are mostly oblivious to what has happened in the outside world, the friends share a look between them that speaks volumes as to the disconnect between the people they have become and the world they are returning to.

In fact, for Frodo, the Shire will never be what it once was. He has come home with scars that will never heal, at least not in the Shire. He is too changed to be able to stay, and ultimately decides he must leave. As devastating as this decision is to the others, especially Sam, we as an audience understand Frodo's choice, and know that he is making the right decision. Frodo, like the Square Peg, cannot fit back into the Round Hole of the Shire, and must set out to find peace somewhere else.

Returning to Sam, he is a powerful example of the Bridge form of the Return. Back at the beginning of the *Fellowship of the Ring* (two movies prior), we see a much different version of Sam. He is shy, timid, and afraid to ask Rosie Cotton to dance. By the end of the third movie, Sam has changed a great deal.

Our first indication of this change is his willingness to finally approach Rosie—something he would not have done before. Sam feels the same friction that they all do upon returning to the Shire, but he is able to use the changes he experienced to carve out a new role for himself. Sam bridges the gap by building a family, an identity, and a place within the community, that is a direct result of the Journey. Where he could not muster up courage before, now he can.

These three different versions of the Return are broad generalizations, but the principles boil down to the same representations. What is interesting about all three versions of the Return is that they are centered on helping the Hero to maintain the person that they have become because of the Journey. The character has paid a great price for who they are now. Their ability to honor both their own Transformation as well as the Gifts they received have a great impact on how their Journey ends.

*"Depending on what we experienced on our Journey,
we may be vastly different than when we left."*

THE JOURNEY AS A CYCLE

Regardless of which version the Hero experiences, the end of one Journey does not mean the ultimate end. Once they reach the end of one story, they have positioned themselves to get called on their next Journey. The process is a cycle, each iteration building upon the previous ones as the Hero continues to grow and change.

This is why we have sequels, trilogies, and more: the Hero is never done progressing. There is always something new to do, some learning that can happen, some new way for the Hero to contribute to the betterment of themselves and the world around them.

Before You Move On:

What types of Returns can you identify? Think of different stories and see if you can pinpoint which of the three (or combination of the three) the Hero experiences. What factors influence the type of Return they experience?

REAL-WORLD JOURNEYS

Alan Cumming's experience growing up was far from ideal. Tormented and abused, Alan struggled well into adulthood with the physical, emotional, and mental damage that became the cost of having a relationship with Alex Cumming, his father.

In his memoir <u>Not My Father's Son</u>, Alan recounts the experience of being invited to participate in a television show to discover more about his ancestry, particularly a grandfather that Alan never knew. The experience leads us through a Journey of emotional devastation and the subsequent healing that came through Alan finding himself strong enough to break out of the abusive relationship and embrace happiness.

As the book concludes, Alan takes his brother and his mother on a celebratory trip to the place where his grandfather had served in the Scottish military and had died, far from home. It is a beautiful, healing trip for the three of them, representing the culmination of all that they had experienced at the hands of Alan's father and the triumph they had achieved in freeing themselves from his influence.

After Alan recounts what he thought would be the end of the story, there is a postscript. Because of a death in the family, he returns to Scotland and, ultimately, to the estate where he had grown up. The experience is full of emotion for Alan, both good and bad, as he finds his father's absence the most prevalent feeling. That absence allowed Alan to finally view his childhood as he would "a box of old photos" he might have accidentally stumbled upon.

As he walks around the different landmarks from his childhood memories, he reflects on how the estate, like he himself, has changed over the years. As both he and the estate were now free of his father's influence, there was a chance to see, and to be, something more than ever before.

"I felt so free. Isn't that funny? I felt at home and happy. This was not an emotion I had ever expected to feel that day." (Not My Father's Son, p. 288)

As I mentioned in the introduction, The Return was the part of the Journey that first opened my eyes to how this information can help people trying to live normal, everyday lives. It's not just literary heroes that have to deal with coming home.

Much like in literature, there are basically three ways that The Return phase can manifest, though in real life there seems to be some fluidity. Often coming home initially looks a lot like the "happily ever after" version, since we were missed and people are very glad to see us. Parties ensue, kind words are exchanged, and we get to revel in the joy of the familiar. It's not until a few days later that the cracks start to show, and expectations meet reality.

For so many of us, we dream that our "return home" will be seamless. Unfortunately, this is rarely the case. Even in the best of circumstances there is some friction as we and those left at home become reacquainted. Depending on what we experienced on our Journey, we may be vastly different than when we left. And while we viewed the entire process and know how things progressed, those at home were not witnesses to it. They don't really know how we went from A to B to C to D; all they know is that we used to be A, and now we're D, and they don't know what that means for them or for the relationship.

To be honest, this can be a threatening experience. It doesn't seem like it should be, but there are people and situations for whom our new, transformed self threatens who they are, or the life they are living. Even if the threat is not consciously perceived, people can react defensively, even aggressively, toward the person we have become.

This isn't because they are evil people, or that they don't care about us. More likely, they have their own Journey that they have avoided going on, and we may be a reminder of that. Ours is not to judge others or their Journey process, but to be aware that the reactions of others may have much more to do with who they are meant to become than it does with who we have become.

We looked at "Sully" Sullenberger when we spoke of Mentors, but he had a very interesting Return after his Unique Task of landing a passenger plane in the Hudson River. For him, stepping out from behind the scenes to become a public figure was a difficult process. In his words,

> *I've become a recipient of people's reflections because I am now the public face of an unexpectedly uplifting moment that continues to resonate. Hearing from so many people, paying attention to their stories—that's part of my new job.*
>
> *I've come to see their thankfulness as a generous gift, and I don't want to diminish their kind words by denying them. Though it made me uncomfortable at first, I've made a decision to graciously accept people's thanks. At the same time, I don't strive to take it as my own. I recognize that I*

have been given a role to play, and maybe some good can happen as a result.

(*Highest Duty*, p. 260)

I find the words that he uses interesting. Sully's reference to his "new job" and being given "a role to play" is an example of the Bridge version of the Return. Landing a plane on the Hudson made him the "public face of an unexpectedly uplifting moment," and forced Sully to make a decision. He could continue to push away those who wanted to interact with him, go back to being something of an unknown (although that was probably impossible), or he could find a way to think differently about these experiences and how he could function in the larger narrative.

For him, this new role that would create that Bridge required him to act in ways that were not natural for him. He found a way to overcome that discomfort by realizing that the incident was much larger than himself. Coming to this conclusion could easily have taken a Journey cycle of its own, but his words suggest that he has figured out his new place, his new "role" within society, and is functioning in that new role.

The extreme nature of the experience of US Airways Flight 1549 allows us to hear Sully describe what his Return experience was like. Not all Journeys have such a visible outcome. For most of us, the processing that happens after our Return is much more subtle, and the results may not be seen until looking back from a distance.

For Alan Cumming, his literal coming home, his ability to face the physical location of his childhood abuse, was an outward manifestation of the inward changes that had happened over the years. He was able to embrace the person he became, to see the progress he had made, and to honor his past without letting it control him.

In a powerful way, Alan demonstrates one of the gifts that the Return can offer: perspective. There are times when we have gone through an experience and can gain perspective quickly on what has occurred; other times it takes longer. Moving through subsequent Journeys may enable that perspective, or it may refine it. Being able to see for ourselves the change between our beginning baseline and our transformed self is a valuable gift indeed.

FINDING MEANING IN CHANGE

After becoming "a little bit famous" following the success of *The Office* and *The Mindy Project*, Mindy Kaling described how the level of fame she was experiencing had changed her. First, she enumerated the things that she can and can't do because other people are now watching, and what she now does because of it.

What I was drawn to as I read her musings was the final paragraph of this thoughtful chapter. She writes:

> *The single best outcome of my (minor) fame is that women— usually young women who feel marginalized for some reason—come up to me, or write to me, to tell me I make them feel more "normal." That is profoundly moving to me. I'm not saying I'm some kind of pioneer here...but I love that. I'm a role model now. It makes all the stuff I can't do anymore completely worth it. It's actually the way that my (minor) fame has changed me the most. I want to be a better person because I don't want to disappoint those girls. I stop and think about my actions more. I tip great, I try not to swear too much, and I remember to thank people and be grateful. And all that stuff I do to "appear" better has actually made me a better person. I wish I had always acted like I was a little bit famous.*

(*Why Not Me?*, p. 47-48)

Mindy's new role as a "minorly" famous person had caused her to examine the way she behaved. In her case, those changes were for the better, and her new role allows her to make a difference in ways that she had not planned or even really thought about as she pursued her dream.

The fame presented her with a choice, and she opted to let this new role change her. Making that choice may have not been an easy transition, as change is difficult for all of us. Making that choice may have required its own Journey cycle. The end result is that she found a way to still be Mindy, but to do so in a way that allows her to fill a new role that improves the world around her and brings her joy and fulfillment.

THE REALITY OF CHANGE

Each of us has experiences that lead us to one of the three possible Return outcomes. For most of us, the Bridge is a combination of the most realistic and most positive outcome. Being aware of the work that is needed can help us to face the realities of Returns that are not always pleasant.

One of the best things that can happen in this transition period is for all parties involved to commit to becoming reacquainted. We are not the same, they are not the same, and taking the time to get to "re-know" each other allows for the best possible outcome. Depending on the length of the separation, the amount of contact there was during the absence, and the degree of change that was made, this may be simple or complex.

Regardless, a change has occurred. Some of the unsung casualties of the sacrifice made in the Abyss are things you had in your life that were dependent upon who you were at the beginning of the Journey. The life you lived before the Journey was a direct interplay between the world around you and the person you were. As that person no longer exists, those things cannot exist in the same way either, and that includes relationships.

Think of it like there needs to be a grieving process for the relationships we had that can no longer exist in the same form. Doing so allows us to be able to embrace the new, and often better, relationships yet to come.

DIFFERENT WAYS OF LEAVING

For the girls I work with at the treatment center, returning home from treatment often means ending relationships with people who want them to go back to their destructive ways. They have to "leave" the previously known relationships in order to maintain the changes they have worked so hard to achieve. In some cases, "leaving" means avoiding certain activities that can be dangerously triggering.

Leaving doesn't mean we have to pack up and move out. It does mean that we need to take a careful look at what influences in our life are supporting our new, transformed self, and those which are not. Once we have identified these, we can determine if a Bridge reaction is the most appropriate, or if leaving is the only way to maintain the Hero we have become.

Before You Move On:

How might you have experienced Returns in your life? Take some time to think about the experiences you have had and write about them. You can use these questions as a guide if you need them:

- What gifts did you receive as a result of the Journey?
- Were they internal? External? Both?
- Which of the three versions of the Return did you experience?
- How did others react to your Return?
- What did you do to handle the experience?

---

10. THANKS, BUT NO THANKS

You want a prediction about the weather, you're asking the wrong Phil. I'll give you a winter prediction: It's gonna be cold, it's gonna be grey, and it's gonna last you for the rest of your life.

—Phil Connors, in *Groundhog Day* by Harold Ramis

We've made it all the way through the Journey Model, making connections to literature and to our own lives. But wait! Might there be some stories that don't follow the Model? Might there be some Heroes whose stories don't go according to the plan? As you might expect, there are.

Variations to the Journey Model happen in the two steps that the Hero has some control over: The Call and The Abyss. These are the two choice points in the stories, and because of that the Hero can choose how they want to proceed. The next two chapters deal with those choices, and the consequences that those choices entail.

TOO HAPPY TO ANSWER

Let's start by looking at characters who reject their Call to begin their Journey. For most characters, the beginning of the story sees them unhappy and listless, willing to accept an Invitation or respond well to a Mandate. Some characters, however, are actually quite happy with their lives. In fact, they are so happy that they don't want anything to change. Ever. If they could, they would freeze everything in that moment so that none of their happiness would ever change.

For characters like this, when the Call comes to them, they reject it for fear of losing their happiness. They have no desire to leave and do something that will change them, as what they want most is to avoid change.

Most of us can see the problem with this mentality. While we all resist change to some degree, attempting to completely avoid change is a rather ridiculous proposition. Change is going to come. For characters in these stories, just as in our lives, there is a purpose behind the change. Destiny is interested in the Hero becoming a better version of themselves.

The Journey that Garion (the main character in Terry Brooks' *Pawn of Prophecy*) takes begins while he is living on a farm. Life is quiet there, and simple, and Garion feels loved and safe. All he has known his whole life is the world of farm, his Aunt Pol, and the predictable patterns of farm life. Things could not be better.

When Garion learns that he is destined for greater things and that his Journey is about to begin, instead of being excited about the prospect, Garion is angry. He feels betrayed that his Aunt Pol is actually a powerful sorceress, he despises the thought of leaving the farm, and he has just started a relationship with a local girl named Zubrette, whom he has no desire to be away from. Given the choice, Garion would put his world back to where it was before he found out the truth and would keep it that way forever. While this would neither serve him nor the world he is prophesied to save, the thought of change is repulsive to him.

As much as most characters are unhappy before their Journeys start, there are those characters who actually are happy. The only problem is that their happiness is dependent on things staying the same. Watch for those characters that don't want anything to change—they are asking for change to come their way.

TOO MISERABLE TO ANSWER

Another version of this alternate starting point would be characters who are miserable, but actually like it that way. These characters find a perverse pleasure in being angry, grumpy, the victim, etc. They are not happy, and that is just fine with them. If accepting the Call would mean giving up this part of their personality, their identity, then they have no interest in it whatsoever. For these characters, just as the characters who are genuinely happy, they would reject a Call that comes to them.

My favorite example of this is Phil Connors from the movie *Groundhog Day*. Phil is a sarcastic, bitter, miserable character, and he loves it. He relishes it. He makes snide remarks, rolls his eyes, mutters insults under his breath, and shows absolutely no signs of stopping.

Given the chance to voluntarily change his negative behavior, Phil would reject it. As other characters in the same boat, Phil sees nothing wrong with what he is doing. The fact that his behavior drives everyone else away is proof that he does not need them anyway. For characters like this, Destiny will only tolerate their negative influence on the world for so long.

DESTINY DOES NOT TAKE "NO" FOR AN ANSWER

Rejecting a Call is an interesting proposition. As Destiny is the driving force behind these Journeys, it has an interest in the Hero changing for the better. Fortunately (though it may feel unfortunate) for a character who rejects the Call, Destiny is going to extend that Call again. And

*"A rejected Call means that the next time that
the Call comes, it is a little bit louder,
a little more intense."*

again. And again. Each and every time, the Hero has the opportunity once again to accept the Call.

The unique aspect of the Call interaction between Destiny and the Hero is that each time there is an invitation that is rejected, the intensity level of the next Call increases.

Generally speaking, the Call begins as something rather subtle or quiet. Perhaps it is a thought, or an off-handed comment, or a growing awareness. A rejected Call means that the next time that the Call comes, it is a little bit louder, a little more intense. Rejected once again, the next Call becomes even louder and even more intense. Ultimately, Destiny is practically yelling at the Hero that it is time to step out the door.

In spite of Destiny presenting a Call that is undeniable, there are characters that will refuse until the end. Reading about this type of character would be frustrating, as there would be no progress and, ultimately, no real interest for us to continue reading.

If a character refuses to accept a Call, and would continue to do so, Destiny will eventually become impatient and force the Hero out the door and across the Threshold. It seems rather harsh, but this is the reality.

These characters are similar to my friend's dog who, upon discovering that it is time for a bath, becomes suddenly faster and smarter than any human being in its quest to avoid getting wet. My friend, knowing that the bath is necessary, will push, pull, drag, and coerce in whatever way is necessary to get him clean.

Destiny is not afraid to do the same. If the character won't leave their house, the house might become damaged in an earthquake or a fire, forcing them to leave. If a character doesn't want to face their faults, those faults end up on the front page of the newspaper. Destiny is a harsh companion when pushed, and it apparently has access to the powers of the universe. Granted, the Journey will be for their good, but that doesn't matter to a reluctant Hero.

Continuing with the example of Phil Connors, we can see how Destiny is forced to step in. I would guess that, in the larger narrative of Phil's life (that would exist before the narrative of the movie), he was given opportunities to act differently. At the point where we meet Phil, his behavior is set and shows no sign of stopping.

Phil, as a character, would never choose to stop acting the way he is acting. So, Destiny intervenes in such a stark, undeniable way that he has no choice but to go on the Journey—in this case, the Journey of living the same day over and over and over. Destiny grabs Phil by the collar and drags him across the Threshold, leaving behind the Known World of living each day only once, to the Unknown World of repeating the same day over and over. He has no choice at that point; he gave up that control with all the previous refusals.

There are other characters who act in a similar fashion. Many of them are comedic characters: their antics amuse us and make us laugh. However, that does not make them immune to the need for change. When a character has reached a level of obstinance in the face of change, Destiny gets impatient. An impatient Destiny is a force to be reckoned with.

MAKING UP FOR LOST TIME

There is one other interesting thing about refused Calls and intensity. It is not just the Calls that become more intense each time they are rejected. Each time a character refuses a Call, the more intense the rest of the Journey becomes as well. Think of it as Destiny having to make up for lost time. The longer the Hero waits to accept the Call, the less time Destiny has to prepare the Hero for what is to come. Therefore, the trials, the temptations, and the sacrifice are much more intense than they would have been had the Call been heeded earlier.

THE SLIGHTLY ALTERED INVITATION

As we are talking about repeated invitations, there are many stories where the form the Call takes will not necessarily be the same each time the Call is extended. A character who is given the opportunity to go on a humanitarian trip in one iteration of the Call, may be presented with a completely different form the next time, like caring for their dying father. This difference must be understood in the context of what the true point of the Journey is: the transformation of the character. These inner transformations can happen in a variety of circumstances.

If the Journey this particular Hero is being called on has the purpose of helping them to become more empathetic (a very common purpose of Journeys), whether the character learns empathy while traveling in a third-world country or learns it while taking care of an elderly relative, the point is the empathy, not the venue in which it is learned. So, while refusing a Call can, in some ways, lead to a lost opportunity that may never come back, more important is the deeper meaning for the Journey and the realization that Destiny has a much larger plan in mind. Opportunities for self-improvement always come again.

Call refusals are not uncommon in everyday living. Part of the reason is the fact that we are surrounded each and every day by hundreds of people wanting our attention. Whether it is the people directly around us (family, friends, co-workers) or people who are paid to try to get our attention (advertisers and businesses), we are bombarded with messages that are filled with urgent calls to action. It would be impossible for us to respond to each and every one, though many of us try. Sifting through these messages and determining which to act upon is a skill that must be developed.

LEARNING TO LISTEN

Recognizing the Call is the first step, and that involves learning how to listen for them. Yes, a million people want our attention, our time, and our money, but only certain nudges are going to be leading us forward toward becoming the best possible version of ourselves.

Prioritizing the thoughts and nudges that we have relating to those closest to us (i.e. spending more time with our kids, sending a kind message to a friend, determining to be a better spouse, etc.) should rank at the top of the list. Not only are these people important to us, but we are most likely playing an active role in their Journeys as Helpers and/or Mentors, just as they are playing a role in ours. In this sense, we get double the results from accepting these Calls.

Listening also involves noticing patterns and persistence in the messages we receive. Like the friend I mentioned in Chapter 2 who had the desire to begin drawing again, we often have a similar emotional reaction to certain Calls that can be a clue that we are being given multiple opportunities to respond. We can feel for some time that a change is either desired or necessary. That "some time" doesn't have to be a long time; it is often just enough time that we know we have felt that way before and haven't acted on it yet. The sooner we recognize and acknowledge those messages that are true Calls, the sooner we can react.

LEARNING TO ACT

The second step, then, is acting on Calls once we recognize them. This is where human nature can be a beast to overcome. For those of us that are particularly adept at making excuses, our skills absolutely shine when it comes to answering Calls that we don't want to accept. We are too busy, too tired, too poor, too weak, too unprepared, and any number of other reasons why "now" is not the time.

In the end, however, excuses are just that: excuses. They tend to ring more and more hollow over time. Deep down, we sense that the reality has nothing to do with what we tell ourselves and more to do with a deep, abiding fear.

Fear is one of the few disabling emotions that we experience, which is why I believe that fear is the major emotion that stops us from moving forward. We are paralyzed by it. Knowing that we are feeling fear is important, particularly if recognizing the emotion is difficult. Acting, even when we feel afraid, can be just as, if not more, difficult.

My own relationship with fear is a complex one. While I'm getting better at recognizing fear as the root cause of much of my inaction, taking those first steps in the face of that fear often requires a series of pep talks. Many times it requires reframing the entire experience, seeing myself as someone who acts in the face of fear instead of being paralyzed by it. How you experience and respond to fear is an understanding worth taking the time to develop.

Learning to listen and learning to act are the keys to answering the Calls that come into our lives. Accepting a Call means going on a Journey—something that we know very well may not be easy. Refusing a Call until Destiny feels the need to drag us across the Threshold may be making it harder than it needs to be.

Before You Move On:

Take some time today to listen to the different Calls that come your way. What type of Calls are they? Can you narrow down the Calls into those that seem the most in tune with your Journeys? What is one Call that you could answer today that would make a difference in your life?

11. NOTHING WILL COME OF NOTHING

Kramer: You know, the important thing is that you learned something.

Jerry: No, I didn't!

— *"The Secret Code"* by Jerry Seinfeld

We've discussed the first of the two variations where Heroes can make a choice: the Call. The Call involves an interplay between the Hero and Destiny where both have power to act. This chapter is going to deal with the variation that is completely about the Hero: a failed Abyss. A refused Call is more a matter of the Hero "choosing" the intensity of the experience they are going to go through. A failed Abyss is a different matter entirely.

WHICH WAY?

As a character reaches their Abyss, they are given a choice. They can either sacrifice whatever the Journey requires for them to be transformed, or they can refuse to make the sacrifice. Chapter 6 was all about what happens when the Hero chooses to make the sacrifice, and the benefits and opportunities that the choice presents.

We can learn a lot by closely examining what happens to the characters who, when faced with the chance to change, deliberately choose not to. In this case, they are consciously choosing to continue their old, prohibitive behavior because they aren't willing to deal with the difficulty of making changes.

Now, they do not do this blindly. The Hero is very aware of how their behavior is unhelpful at least, destructive at worst. And yet, the thought of having to give up that part of themselves is more than they are willing to accept, especially if this behavior has defined them.

For characters who hit the Abyss moment and choose not to make the sacrifice, the result is that instead of moving forward on their Journey, they move backward. In fact, they move back to the beginning of the cycle. Any progress that they may have made will, at least for now, be lost.

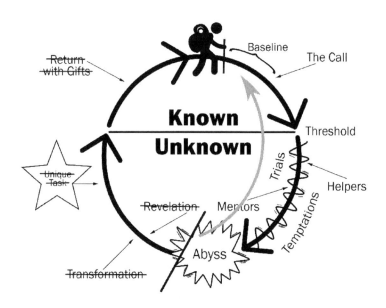

THREE-DIMENSIONAL PROGRESS

A failed Abyss is particularly harmful because, if you take the cycle and turn it on its side, you can more easily see that each successful, subsequent iteration sees the Hero progressing upward. They are not cycling on the same plane over and over; each complete cycle moves them up to a new plane of existence. A failed Abyss, therefore, not only takes them back to the beginning, it takes them back down to their original plane of existence.

Some stories deal with characters who hit this choice point and not only choose regression once, they do so over and over. Destiny continues to extend a Call, the Hero accepts the Call, they work their way through the Trials to the Abyss, but each and every time they arrive at the moment of choice, they choose their old habits. Again. And again. And again. We actually have a name for these types of stories. We call them Tragedies.

THE TRAGIC TALE

Tragic characters are always given the choice to do things differently, but they do not accept those opportunities. You may have experienced discussions about "tragic flaws," particularly relating to characters from ancient Greek writings, where the character was born a certain way, and is somehow destined to act a certain way. Contrary to the way these qualities are presented, those flaws are not insurmountable.

We may act like that is "just the way the character is," but the point of Journeys is that they don't have to be that way. They can change. The characters simply choose not to change the way they behave or react. There is nothing the Journey asks of them that is impossible strictly because of who a character is; there is only the willingness of the Hero to accept the opportunity given to them.

To find examples of tragic characters, Shakespeare is certainly the first author to come to mind. Othello, in particular, embodies this type of failed Abyss. Over and over he is given the chance to listen to his wife Desdemona, to trust her, to accept that she is telling him the truth. Over and over, he allows his own insecurities to destroy their relationship.

Choosing to trust his wife in the face of the "evidence" that Iago presents about Desdemona's infidelity may seem like a difficult thing to do, but the reward of being married to a faithful, loyal wife would have been worth it. Tragically, he allows his insecurity to lead to the destruction of his happiness and the murder of his wife. Othello could have chosen differently.

We see tragic characters in modern times as well. I believe that one of the great American tragedies of all time is actually a television show most people wouldn't consider a tragedy: Seinfeld.

When people think of Seinfeld, they think of comedy. These are characters who made people laugh over and over and over. If you stop to think about it, however, these are characters who, when presented with the opportunity to change, chose their same behaviors— selfishness, pettiness, and greed—every single time.

In fact, that was the whole point of the show; Jerry Seinfeld and Larry David were adamant that the characters would not learn and grow. (The unofficial mantra of the show was "No hugs. No learning.") While entertaining on the screen, if these were people in our own lives, they would be difficult to associate with on a long-term basis.

BALANCED OPTIONS

When describing the Abyss earlier, I talked briefly about the fact that the choice presented in the Abyss must be balanced. The choice to

"What seems like a clear choice when we are not in the moment becomes intensely difficult to make when the time to choose actually arrives."

sacrifice must be just as tempting as the choice to retain. This makes it different from The Call where Destiny may step in and force the character over the Threshold.

In the case of the Abyss, Destiny cannot force the character to a successful Abyss. That would defeat the entire purpose of the Abyss.

The sacrifice must be a willing one, or the character will not transform. If they do not transform, they cannot accomplish their Unique Task because they won't meet those unique requirements. Destiny must, therefore, allow the character to fail at the Abyss over and over. Doing otherwise would be futile.

For this reason, we have stories that break our hearts as we watch a character who has the chance to do things differently, to have the opportunities and victories that await them on the other side of the Abyss, but they choose not to take advantage of that chance. Over. And over. The loss is devastating for the character, and for the audience as well. But no one can save them from themselves; the choice and subsequent result is ultimately theirs and theirs alone.

REAL-WORLD JOURNEYS

A failed Abyss is serious business. On a personal level, we are rejecting an opportunity to change and become better than we were before. However, a failed Abyss does not make for a tragic end. Tragedies only happen if we continue to reject the opportunity to change, knowingly retaining a part of ourselves that is prohibitive, harmful, or even destructive. In other words, if you are able to identify a failed Abyss that you have experienced, that is not the end of the story.

THE HOPE IN THE HEARTACHE

Our second son has, from the time he was little, disliked vegetables. Not all vegetables, but most vegetables. When we put a meal in front of him that has a vegetable in it, he decides ahead of time that he isn't going to like it. This happens over and over at dinner, since we try to incorporate vegetables into our meals as much as possible.

You'd think this was a story about our son missing the opportunity to try new things, but it is actually a story about me. You see, each time this scenario takes place, I am given a choice about how to react. Unfortunately, I keep reacting in the same, frustrated way. This leads to tension and frustration between us. The situation comes up, I react the same way, we leave dinner frustrated.

Now, I can tell myself that a) I want what is best for my son, and b) that learning to eat vegetables will greatly improve his health, and c) that he needs to get out of his head about the vegetables and d) try them without deciding that he doesn't like them first.

Clearly this is a script I have told myself enough that it is second nature. Knowing that it is a script doesn't mean that what I'm telling myself isn't true. The point, though, is that if I keep reacting the same way, it is going to damage my relationship with my son.

There are other ways I can react, other tactics, other modes of communication, that will lead to a much healthier conversation, but I have to choose to change the way I am reacting. More importantly, I have to make that choice in the moment when emotions may be elevated and well-worn patterns of behavior are fighting back. What seems like a clear choice when we are not in the moment becomes intensely difficult to make when the time to choose actually arrives.

Acting in a way that is contrary to our well-traveled paths of behavior is not easy. Our attempts often come out awkward and uncomfortable, and that can cause doubt whether or not it is worth trying to change.

Let us consider the alternative, however. If we continue with the previous behavior, we not only fail to progress personally, but we are also choosing behavior that often hurts those around us. Only we can decide how the story will turn out, and ultimately, we will have to own our part in those decisions.

TURNING AROUND AT THE END

In discussing the different forms a Return can take, I mentioned one of the factors contributing to the experience is the commitment of the Hero to maintain the changes they have experienced on their Journey. This commitment is what creates friction with those the Hero returns to, and sometimes this friction is more than the Hero can take.

Let me be clear: almost every Hero returns home with a commitment to maintain the changes they have experienced. They have seen the other side of the Abyss, they've had a Revelation and Transformation, and they know that these changes are crucial for their happiness.

However, sometimes the friction is so intense that the Hero determines that giving up the changes is the only way to stop the anguish and frustration. While this is more an issue of perspective and the ability to see alternatives, we must acknowledge that maintaining changes in the face of resistance is exhausting and can overwhelm us.

Giving up our Transformation sees us with the same result as a failed Abyss: we return to the beginning of the Journey. It would be nice if we only had to go back a little bit and then move forward again, but that doesn't seem to be how it works. A new Call is extended, Trials and Temptations experienced, Abyss choices made, etc. We go through the cycle again.

However, because we did make it past the Abyss before, we were Transformed in some way. As much as we go back to the beginning, we don't go back as the same person we were before. This is hopeful, because it means we can take what we learned and, potentially, move through the Trials and Temptations more quickly and identify the Abyss more readily because we can see with our new perspective.

The main point of understanding a failed Abyss or an abandoned

Transformation is to know that these are not terminal. We will get another chance to make a different decision. We have the capability to do things differently. Recognizing not only what has happened, but our own ability to do something about it, makes us more powerful than we give ourselves credit for. The end of our story is up to us.

Before You Move On:

Can you identify an area of your life where you might be stuck in this "tragic" cycle? Are there arguments you keep having, situations you keep avoiding, changes you want to make but keep backing away? Take some time to write about those experiences. Is there something you might do differently the next time you have the chance?

---

12. LET ME CLARIFY THIS

It is not the critic who counts; not the man who points out how the strong man stumbles, or where the doer of deeds could have done them better. The credit belongs to the man who is actually in the arena, whose face is marred by dust and sweat and blood; who strives valiantly; who errs, who comes short again and again, because there is no effort without error and shortcoming; but who does actually strive to do the deeds; who knows great enthusiasms, the great devotions; who spends himself in a worthy cause; who at the best knows in the end the triumph of high achievement, and who at the worst, if he fails, at least fails while daring greatly, so that his place shall never be with those cold and timid souls who neither know victory nor defeat.
—Teddy Roosevelt

Before we wrap up our time together, I want to mention five final truths about this process that are crucial to living the Journey to its full potential.

1. PREDICTABILITY IS NOT SIMPLICITY

The first is knowing that this process, while predictable, is never simple. Trying to figure out where you are in a given Journey cycle can be very difficult because we are, at any given time, at various stages in various cycles.

Our lives are a series of cycles that overlap. That means we are, simultaneously, living different parts of the process for different parts of our lives. You may be deciding whether or not to respond to a Call to spend more time with your children, while simultaneously experiencing the Trials and Tribulations of a new assignment at work. Add to that the Abyss you are experiencing trying to kick a bad habit, as well as the stress of preparing for your pickleball tournament this Saturday, and life gets to be pretty complex.

Not only are you living several cycles at the same time, each larger cycle is made up of multiple smaller cycles. You may experience an entire Journey cycle just to be ready to accept a Call. Each Trial that you go through may require a cycle in and of itself. The stories we read rarely get that complex, as the point is to tell a larger, more

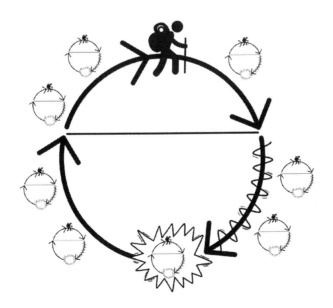

encompassing story. Life, however, means that you may experience a full cycle every day, maybe even multiple times a day, just on a very small, focused scale.

In the classroom, I am asking students to participate in the process of learning—something that very closely resembles the patterns of the Journey Model. My focus is very much limited to the concepts I am teaching or the skills I'm trying to help them develop, but I do so with full knowledge that school is a small component in the larger picture of their lives.

By the time I see them in class, I am stepping into the middle of their day. Sometimes there can be a particular cycle in their individual lives that overwhelms them to the point of impeding other cycles, including the ones I have planned for class. This is one of the struggles of life: learning to balance all the different places and ways that life is making demands of us. Knowing this does not make it any easier, but understanding the complexity allows us to cut ourselves a little slack. This is no easy feat we are trying to accomplish.

2. YOUR JOURNEY IS UNIQUE

What you are experiencing in this series of Journeys is a one-of-a-kind endeavor. No one has ever had the same Calls, Trials, Abysses, Tasks, etc., as you.

There are, of course, good things and bad things about this truth. First and foremost, no one else can tell us how to live our Journey. It is meant for us, for the person *we* are, for the person *we* are meant to become, and not anyone else. That means that the conclusions and decisions and Revelations others have experienced are not necessarily applicable to our situation, no matter how much they would like them to be. We must find the truth, the insight, the sacrifices, and the paths for ourselves.

This is not to discount the wisdom and knowledge of others (i.e.

Helpers and Mentors). Others may give their opinions and thoughts, and those can be crucial helps along the way. But there is no one single path toward the end of the story. What is right for one person's Journey may not be right for another's or may not be right for them at the moment. Timing is an incredibly complex factor in this process. Acknowledging that there are universal truths to be learned, the order we learn them in and the work it takes to learn them is unique to us.

The flip side is that we cannot count on others to be able to tell us which way to go all of the time. They don't know; they only know their own Journeys. We have to be the ones to make the final decision, and that can create a great deal of uncertainty. We like knowing what is coming, how it is going to turn out, and exactly what we are supposed to do—or at least know whom to blame.

All too often we want the ability to choose, unless that choice is going to end poorly. Then we want someone else to choose for us. We cannot have it both ways. The Universe has allowed us the ability to choose; how we use that power us up to us. The result of the Journey is ours alone, whether we want it or not. We have to own both the freedom and the responsibility, the success and the failure, the joy and the sorrow. In so doing, we can finally become whole.

This beautiful, messy, difficult, wonderful process is creating the story of a lifetime, and we get to determine (in many ways) what that story will be.

3. JOURNEYS ARE UNIVERSAL EXPERIENCES

As much as we are in the middle of trying to successfully complete our own Journey cycles, at some point we have to acknowledge that the person texting during a movie, the guy that cut us off while driving, the co-worker who seems bent on making our lives harder, are all experiencing Journeys of their own.

Everyone experiences Journeys. Everyone. All of us have times when we handle them well; all of us have times when we handle them poorly. Knowing that everyone is on a Journey of some kind means that we all have a lot more in common than we may think.

While it is true that no one else has had the same experiences we have, and maybe they can't understand the specifics of our personal Journey, they have been on Journeys. They relate to the listlessness of the beginning and feel the pull of a Call. They know the fear of stepping across the Threshold and the frustration of the Trials and Temptations. They have felt the despair of the Abyss, and the joy of coming out the other side and accomplishing something great. They have all gone home, preparing for yet another Journey.

The Journey experience brings us together in ways that almost nothing else can. The sooner we see others as fellow travelers (who may actually need our support), the sooner we can start cutting each other some slack and respond with more empathy and compassion. Their struggles echo in ours. Their failed Abysses speak to our own failures. Perhaps at this moment they are stumbling and we are not; at some point those roles will be reversed. More reason, then, to reach down and help someone up—we may need them do the same for us someday.

As the last stanza in Sam Walter Foss' poem "The House by the Side of the Road" declares,

Let me live in my
house by the side of the road
Where the race of men go by-
They are good, they are bad, they are weak, they are strong,
Wise, foolish- so am I.
Then why should I sit in the scorner's seat
Or hurl the cynic's ban?-
Let me live in my house by the side of the road
And be a friend to man.

4. JOURNEYS FOLLOW A PATH TOWARD VIRTUE

Understanding the Journey cycle as a universal, shared experience is an important part of why learning about it matters. But, figuring how our individual Journeys fit into the larger scheme of things is sometimes difficult. The end result isn't always obvious, at least not right away. We can feel like we are spinning our wheels or wasting our time, though neither may actually be true. So how does what we are experiencing right now, in this particular Journey, matter?

If you subscribe to a particular religion or philosophy, the Journey process fits into just about every belief system. If you do not connect with a particular organization, the Journey can act as a framework for understanding the larger picture of our lives.

What matters is understanding the larger forces at work, whether you think of those forces as God, the Universe, Destiny, Source, Nature, or any other appropriate name. These outside forces are moral and benevolent, seemingly wanting the best not just for us, but for everyone. The Journeys we experience are influenced by these forces, and are always directed toward developing virtuous characteristics such as wisdom, compassion, kindness, courage, and more, not on any sort of physical or material attainment.

Because the forces are external and seem to have a larger perspective than we do, these Journeys often result in experiences and growth well beyond what we could initially see. Like a wise trainer that knows we are capable of lifting more weight than we think we can, Journeys are shaping us to become more than we think we are capable of becoming.

Trusting in the good of the Journeys, the good in us and others, the good in the forces that drive us forward, allows us to embrace change that may be difficult or painful, but see us becoming more than we could ever imagine.

5. NO MAGIC PILL

At the risk of ending on something of a downer, the last thing we need to talk about is the reality of knowing this information.

Once you have finished this book, your life should become substantially easier, right? Knowing what lies ahead of you, what to expect out of a Journey, should mean that the process will be much smoother, won't it?

Unfortunately, no.

In reading this book I hope you can see why this is the case, but I want to make sure that we manage your expectations. In the world that we live in, full of quick-fixes and skip-to-the-end solutions, it is dangerous for me to admit that what I outline in this book will not, in many ways, make your Journeys any easier.

Knowledge is most definitely power. Knowing that there is a pattern to all of these processes, that there are predictable phases and steps we can recognize and follow, has the potential to vastly change our experience with the Journey. But it cannot change the structure of the Journey itself. This knowledge will not take away struggles, nor will it make choices easier—doing so would defeat the purpose of the Journey we are on. What it will do, however, is change things that we may not have thought about.

Knowing that Journeys are part of the human experience helps us know that we are not alone. Help is not only available, it is an integral part of the process. We must reach out to those around us acting in the roles of Helpers or Mentors, and then be willing to act in those roles for others. The Journey process has built in support for our difficult moments; it is up to us to use it. We are in this together.

Knowing the steps to the process can help put our experiences into perspective. We tried something new and it didn't work? Feeling like we have hit rock bottom and things seem hopeless? There is a major test coming up, and we don't know how it will turn out? What may seem like a string of random events can now be put into a context, a framework, that not only gives experiences meaning, but gives suggestions for how to react to these moments.

Knowing the steps to the process allows us to stop fighting the process, including the major and minor incidents that make up our lives. If we know that choosing to accept a Call is not the end of difficulty, but the beginning of a series of experiences designed to make us better, stronger, and more than we thought we could become, we can stop panicking every time things are hard. Instead, we can settle into the process and, as the Buddha teaches, lean in to the difficulty, knowing that the struggles that come are exactly what we need. If we are honest with ourselves, we know that what we need is much more important than what we want. We have a say in how our story ends, and that understanding is not only powerful, it sets us free.

In the end, the Journey is before us, whether we welcome it or not. To have the courage to face, and embrace, these Journeys with our eyes wide open is the adventure of a lifetime.

"Lean in to the difficulty, knowing that the struggles that come are exactly what we need."

EPILOGUE

You gain strength, courage and confidence by every experience in which you really stop to look fear in the face. You are able to say to yourself, "I lived through this horror. I can take the next thing that comes along." ... You must do the thing you think you cannot do.

—Eleanor Roosevelt

If you've made it to the end, Congratulations! This is a lot to take in, and in many cases can feel like a Journey in and of itself just to make it through the groundwork. There is power in knowing this information, and you may have already seen things differently than you did before.

In the interest of practicality, this book focuses strictly on the foundational principles of understanding the Journey Model. Learning to use this lens can take some time, but the more you practice the more you will be able to recognize the ways your life follows this pattern. Recognition is a sign that the concepts are becoming a part of the way you see the world, and that is powerful indeed.

Being able to recognize the pattern is the first step; knowing what to do with that information is the next. If you are interested in learning more about strategies, practices, and tools that can be applied to different Journey struggles, please visit our website (thejourneyblueprint.com) where you will be able to find additional (and ever-growing) resources that go more in-depth into the Journey and how to live it more fully.

Thank you for allowing me to be a part of your Journey. Feel free to contact me if you have questions, examples, or ideas that you'd like to share!

To download a free printable copy of this template, visit thejourneyblueprint.com.

ACKNOWLEDGEMENTS

The author would like to thank those who have been so supportive on this Journey towards publishing this book.

To Rachel, Johnette, Baxy, and Lisa for being my frontline readers. Your questions and suggestions made all the difference in the world.

To my dear friends and neighbors who let me test these ideas out on them, especially Pam, David, Michelle, Vicki, Lori, Shandy, Lisa, Tressa, Aimee, Emily, Rachel, Kathy, Matt, Kristi, Jewell, and Christi. Your thoughts and questions are all throughout this book.

To Elayne, who has been a cheerleader, friend, mentor, and fellow traveler, pushing me to pursue these ideas for years before I finally listened. Thank you.

To my wonderful parents and supportive siblings and in-laws for not writing me off as crazy. Thank you for encouraging me to keep going.

To my amazing children, for giving me the greatest Journey I could ever have hoped for. You guys make each day a miracle.

And finally, to my best friend and husband. No one has had to hear this more times than you as I tried to figure it all out. Thanks for being on this Journey with me, for constantly supporting me, and for believing in me when I could not. Yours, always.

SOURCE LIST

Angelou, Maya. *The Heart of a Woman*. Random House Trade
   Paperbacks, 2009.

Bradbury, Ray. *Dandelion Wine*. Harper Voyager, 2008.

Brown, Daniel James. *The Boys in the Boat: The True Story of an American
   Teams Epic Journey to Win Gold at the 1936 Olympics*. Viking, 2013.

Campbell, Joseph. *The Hero with a Thousand Faces*. Princeton University
   Press, 1993.

Carson, Ben, and Cecil B. Murphey. *Gifted Hands*. Zondervan
   Publishing House, 1996.

Clements, Ron, et al., directors. *Moana*. Walt Disney Studios Home
   Entertainment, 2017.

Collins, Suzanne. *The Hunger Games*. Scholastic, 2011.

Cumming, Alan. *Not My Fathers Son: A Family Memoir*. Canongate Books
   Ltd, 2015.

Darabont, Frank, director. *The Shawshank Redemption*. Castle Rock
   Entertainment, 2004.

Dweck, Carol S. *Mindset: The New Psychology of Success*. Ballantine Books,
   2008.

Eddings, David. *Pawn of Prophecy*. Ballantine, 1982.

Fey, Tina. *Bossypants*. Little, Brown, 2013.

Frankl, Viktor E. *Man's Search for Meaning: An Introduction to Logotherapy*.
   Pocket Books, 1963.

Harvardgazette. "Text of J.K. Rowling's Speech." *Harvard Gazette*,
   Harvard Gazette, 5 Jan. 2018,
   news.harvard.edu/gazette/story/2008/06/text-of-j-k-rowling-
   speech/.

Huffington, Arianna. *Thrive: The Third Metric to Redefining Success and Creating a Life of Well-Being, Wisdom, and Wonder*. Baker & Taylor, 2015.

Jackson, Peter, director. *The Lord of the Rings: The Return of the King*. New Line Home Entertainment, 2002.

Jackson, Peter, director. *The Lord of the Rings: The Return of the King*. New Line Home Entertainment, 2004.

Kaling, Mindy. *Why Not Me?* CNIB, 2016.

Keller, Helen, et al. *The Story of My Life: the Restored Edition with Her Letters (1887-1901), and a Supplementary Account of Her Education, Including Passages from the Reports and Letters of Her Teacher, Anne Mansfield Sullivan, by John Albert Macy*. Modern Library, 2004.

Lucas, George, director. *Star Wars IV: A New Hope*. Lucas Film Ltd, 1977.

Martel, Yann. *Life of Pi*. Walker Canongate, 2010.

Parekh, Bhikhu C. *Gandhi*. Sterling, 2010.

Pressfield, Steven. *The War of Art*. Rugged Land, 2002.

Rowling, J. K. *Harry Potter and the Sorcerer's Stone*. Arthur A. Levine Books, an Imprint of Scholastic Inc., 2018.

Seinfeld, Jerry, and Larry David. "The Secret Code." *Seinfeld*, 9 Nov. 1995.

Sullenberger, Chesley Burnett, and Jeffrey Zaslow. *Highest Duty: My Search for What Really Matters*.

Tolkien, J. R. R. *Fellowship of the Ring*. HarperCollins, 2007.

Whedon, Joss. "Once More with Feeling." *Buffy the Vampire Slayer*, season 6, episode 7, UPN, 6 Nov. 2001.

Zaloga, Steve, and Steve Noon. *Dwight Eisenhower: Leadership, Strategy, Conflict*. Osprey, 2011.

(This satisfies my English Teacher Inner-Nerd in ways that I just can't explain…)

ABOUT THE AUTHOR

Julie's Journey began in California but she has spent most of her life in Utah where she lives with her best friend/husband Ryan and six amazing kids. She has been an educator for more than 15 years, with experience ranging from students in public, charter, private, and university settings, to pre-service and practicing teachers. She has also had the privilege of running educational groups in therapeutic settings. Her passion for learning and teaching has led her through two Masters degrees: Master of Education in Curriculum and Instruction, and Master of Science in Management and Leadership; the development of multiple professional and personal development courses; and writing. When she isn't pursuing those passions, she loves traveling, playing board games, reading, and watching MST3K with those she loves.

Made in the USA
Columbia, SC
10 August 2020